Developing Accessible iOS Apps

Support VoiceOver, Dynamic Type, and More

Daniel Devesa Derksen-Staats

Apress®

Developing Accessible iOS Apps: Support VoiceOver, Dynamic Type, and More

Daniel Devesa Derksen-Staats
London, UK

ISBN-13 (pbk): 978-1-4842-5307-6   ISBN-13 (electronic): 978-1-4842-5308-3
https://doi.org/10.1007/978-1-4842-5308-3

Managing Director, Apress Media LLC: Welmoed Spahr
Acquisitions Editor: Aaron Black
Development Editor: James Markham
Coordinating Editor: Jessica Vakili

Distributed to the book trade worldwide by Springer Science+Business Media New York, 233 Spring Street, 6th Floor, New York, NY 10013. Phone 1-800-SPRINGER, fax (201) 348-4505, e-mail orders-ny@springer-sbm.com, or visit www.springeronline.com. Apress Media, LLC is a California LLC and the sole member (owner) is Springer Science + Business Media Finance Inc (SSBM Finance Inc). SSBM Finance Inc is a **Delaware** corporation.

For information on translations, please e-mail rights@apress.com, or visit http://www.apress.com/rights-permissions.

Apress titles may be purchased in bulk for academic, corporate, or promotional use. eBook versions and licenses are also available for most titles. For more information, reference our Print and eBook Bulk Sales web page at http://www.apress.com/bulk-sales.

Any source code or other supplementary material referenced by the author in this book is available to readers on GitHub via the book's product page, located at www.apress.com/978-1-4842-5307-6. For more detailed information, please visit http://www.apress.com/source-code.

Printed on acid-free paper

Para Marcos, que puede con todo! 💪!!

Table of Contents

About the Author

Daniel Devesa Derksen-Staats is a passionate developer with a wide variety of experiences in iOS. While at university, he cofounded Desfici, a mobile development company, building in-house projects and also apps for clients, and he hasn't stopped developing for iOS since then. Daniel has worked in start-ups like the social network Bananity and MusicQubed, developing the MTV Trax music app. He has also been part of bigger organizations like the BBC, building the BBC News and BBC+ apps, Skyscanner, and now Spotify. Always trying to embed accessibility in the team's culture, he helps develop more accessible and inclusive apps. Sometimes he lets Xcode have a break and spreads the love for accessibility at conferences, such as AppDevCon in Amsterdam, AltConf in San Jose, SwiftFest in Boston, and MobileConf in Bangkok. You can find him on Twitter as @dadederk.

About the Technical Reviewer

Ahmed Bakir is an iOS author, teacher, and entrepreneur. He has worked on over 30 mobile projects, ranging from advising startups to architecting apps for Fortune 500 companies. In 2014, he published his first book, *Beginning iOS Media App Development*, followed by the first edition of *Program the Internet of Things with Swift for iOS* in 2016 and the second edition in 2018. In 2015, he was invited to develop courses and teach iOS development at UCSD Extension. He is currently building cool stuff in Tokyo! You can find him online at devatelier.com.

Acknowledgments

I've been extremely lucky in my career and I've enjoyed going to work every day, everywhere I've been, and I've learned tons from the people that surrounded me. So I'd like to thank everyone that has shared even a single day of iOS development with me: the research group ARTEC in the University of Valencia; my Desfici cofounders and everyone involved in the development of Unlocked!; the Bananity team; my colleagues from MusicQubed; the BBC News Apps team, the BBC+ team, and the Accessibility Champions at the BBC; to Skyscanner, especially the Vespa squad and the Accessibility Guild; and to my new friends at Spotify and the Spotify Kids team.

Special thanks to Alasdair McCall for helping with the review of the book. To Raúl Gil for designing the amazing illustration at the beginning of the book. And to Marta, without her this book would have been simply impossible.

Also thanks to everyone in Apress that gave me the opportunity to write this book: Aaron Black for suggesting me the idea of writing it in the first place, and Jessica Vakili, James Markham, Nirmal Selvaraj, and Ahmed Bakir for all your help in the edition and technical review of the book.

CHAPTER 1

Introduction

What is accessibility and why is it so important to make our apps accessible? We will start our journey of learning how to build apps for everyone by understanding how diverse your users are, and how to make sure your app works for all of them.

Most of times, when developers don't make their apps accessible, there is a very simple reason behind: they are completely unaware of what accessibility is, what the process of making accessible apps consists of, and how much making accessible apps can positively impact other people's lives.

If you are reading this, it is because you've probably heard about it already, about its power, and you are willing to learn more about it. That's great! Thanks for joining in so we can work together to make more inclusive and accessible apps.

What is accessibility?

So, first things first, what is accessibility exactly? According to the Oxford Dictionary, accessibility is "The quality of being easily reached, entered, or used by people who have a disability" (`https://en.oxforddictionaries.com/definition/accessibility`).

Apple says they tend to think about accessibility as "Making technology usable by everyone" (`https://developer.apple.com/videos/play/wwdc2018/230/`).

© Daniel Devesa Derksen-Staats 2019
D. D. Derksen-Staats, *Developing Accessible iOS Apps*,
https://doi.org/10.1007/978-1-4842-5308-3_1

According to Microsoft, "The qualities that make an experience open to all" (https://download.microsoft.com/download/b/0/d/b0d4bf87-09ce-4417-8f28-d60703d672ed/inclusive_toolkit_manual_final.pdf).

I really like both Apple's and Microsoft's definitions simply because they refer to everyone and all. Take Figure 1-1 as an example. The same way the ramp enables access to everybody, it is clear that making accessible technology is going to make it open to all and usable by everyone.

Figure 1-1. *Accessible solutions benefit everyone (Illustration: Raul-gil.com)*

It is important to be aware that accessibility is not about creating and maintaining a separate simplified version of your app with a subset of functionalities for a specific group of users. That is never a good idea. It is about not excluding anyone from accessing and using the experience you created.

Why accessibility?

We briefly mentioned in the introduction of the chapter that the main reason why some developers don't put some effort in developing accessible apps is probably because they don't really know about it.

But there are other reasons; it could be the case that their managers could not be considering it as something it is worth putting resources on. The same way there might be managers that may not want you to spend time writing tests or doing TDD, or pair programming, etc. If that happens, it is probably due to a lack of understanding of what the benefits those practices bring and how important they are for the team, the business, and the users.

Most developers that want to start making their apps accessible ask themselves the same question: why accessibility? And, how can I convince my team/manager/company we should do it? And the reason should be pretty simple:

> ***"It is just the right thing to do!"***

As Tim Cook also said, "Accessibility rights are human rights." I couldn't agree more with that quote. But for some reason, that doesn't seem to be enough justification for some people, so let's try to explore some other reasons why you should think about accessibility when developing new features.

You want to increase your user base

Any manager wants their app to be used by as many people as possible. That is why we try to launch our apps in a global market like the App Store. And that is why we do things like internationalizing and localizing our apps so that more and more people can understand them and use them. But guess what? By not making your app accessible, you are leaving people out in every single market in which you are making efforts toward acquiring users.

Any developer of an app with an aim of reaching a global audience needs to internationalize and localize the app, and make it accessible. Sometimes the first bit may seem more obvious. But both things are in essence ways of making your app available to more people.

Money

Related to the previous one, it is also pretty obvious, but it is worth remembering that it is a great opportunity. Like in every business, with clients/users comes the possibility of revenue and profit. You might be missing out the money that people with disabilities are willing to spend, but your app is not letting them to. If they find your app, and it works for them, they're more likely to use it over other apps that are not usable for them. And they will tell other users about their great experience too.

Just as an example, in this video from the BBC, "The power of the 'purple' pound," they highlight that the spending power from people of working age that have a disability is reckoned to be worth £249 billion a year to the UK economy: `www.bbc.com/news/av/business-39040760/the-power-of-the-purple-pound-explained`.

It shouldn't be about numbers, but here are some big numbers for you

Managers may want numbers to justify the previous reasons. They may ask you if you can measure that, if you can prove that there are assistive technology users using your app, if you can maybe add some analytics to see if it is worth it. But gathering data around the usage of assistive technologies by your users has a couple of problems: the first one is that it can be unethical to do it – unless you gather this data in an aggregated way so it can't be tracked back to the individual user. The second one is that if your app is not accessible, chances are no one is using your app with a screen reader, for example. The same way that if your app is not in Chinese, you may barely have any users in China. So please don't fall in that trap.

But here are some big numbers for you. According to the World Health Organization, over a billion people – that is, about 15% of the world's population – have some form of disability. And they have a good point: that number is just increasing due to population aging and a rise in chronic health conditions, among other causes (`www.who.int/en/news-room/fact-sheets/detail/disability-and-health`).

Or you may also be surprised to know that 1 in 12 men (more than 8%) has a "red-green" color vision deficiency (also known as color blindness) and the NHS, the National Health Service in the United Kingdom, defines it as "common" (`www.nhs.uk/conditions/colour-vision-deficiency/`). If you are wondering why I just mentioned the numbers for men, it is because, curiously, it is not as common among women, 1 in 200 (0.5%).

Can you afford leaving that many people out of the potential user base of your app?

Legal

You may be legally obliged to develop accessible products. In the United Kingdom, the Equality Act 2010 says that "all UK service providers must make 'reasonable adjustments' for disabled people." And new regulations came into force for public sector bodies on 23 September 2018. They say you must make your web site or mobile app more accessible by making it "perceivable, operable, understandable and robust." And also that: "if someone requests it, provide an accessible alternative within a reasonable time for content that doesn't meet the standards" (`www.gov.uk/guidance/accessibility-requirements-for-public-sector-websites-and-apps`).

In the United States, the Americans with Disabilities Act, known as ADA, "is a civil rights law that prohibits discrimination against individuals with disabilities in all areas" (`https://adata.org/learn-about-ada`).

More recently, the European Union has been working on the EU Directive 2019/882 on the Accessibility Requirements for Products and Services (`https://eur-lex.europa.eu/eli/dir/2019/882/oj`), which will cover for the first time e-books, e-commerce, phones, banking services, etc.

Automation

Automation tools and frameworks like *XCUITest* leverage the accessibility APIs (*UIAccessibility*), so an accessible app can make UI automation easier. For example, if you rely on accessibility identifiers for accessing certain UI components when testing, it will make your UI tests much more reliable than if you use accessibility labels, which are subject to be changed quite often. Good automation tests may increase the confidence in the right functioning of your app, and they may help you release more often and with less overhead. So here you have another benefit of accessibility that you may not have been expecting.

Usability

Making your app accessible can help make your app more usable for everyone. When creating apps with cleaner layouts, bigger and bolder text, higher contrast ratios, etc., it is not just helping users with cognitive needs or low vision, it benefits everyone.

Testing your app with assistive technologies, like VoiceOver, also gives you a new perspective about it. It gives you the opportunity to use your app in a different way because it goes beyond the UI and how it looks, and it puts more emphasis on its structure and how you interact with it instead. A nice-looking app isn't necessarily usable, and accessibility may help you achieve that. Because, would you be able to use your app with your eyes closed? I bet your answer is yes straight away. We'll see how you can do in Chapter 7, and the result might surprise you.

It is very self-rewarding

Did I mention it is the right thing to do? It is also extremely self-rewarding. A few years ago, I used to work in a small startup in Barcelona, Bananity. One day we got a great review in the App Store. Someone wrote a very grateful message thanking the founders of the startup for making the app accessible. Back in the day I didn't know much about accessibility, but for the simple purpose of making my life easier, I used native components as much as possible. And this is the first piece of advice in this book: native UI components will help you easily create accessible apps. The thing is that, to be honest, I don't recall any other reviews we had in the app. But that one made my day and I still remember it today. And more important than anything, it showed me that as a mobile developer, you can make a huge impact on other people's lives by making accessible apps.

It is probably not as complicated as you think. At all

This is probably one of the main reasons why developers may not think about accessibility: they might find it daunting. But trust me, in most cases, it really isn't that complicated. And that is going to be the main purpose of this book: to convince you, so you can convince others, that by knowing just a few basic principles and techniques, and just taking them into account in your day-to-day development process – just the same way you may take into account other things like analytics, testing, documentation, etc. – you can create pretty amazing accessible experiences for your users.

Do you want an Apple Design Award?

It is the most prestigious award an iOS app can get. We've all dreamed with winning one of those one day, right? Well, at one of WWDC 2019 sessions, "Design Award Winning Apps and Games," they explained some of the core aspects they look for in an app or game when considering them for the awards. Among those, you have things like innovation, trust, refinement, aesthetics, attention to detail, and, of course, inclusion. And they talk about how important it is to "design for everyone and investigate if your app is inclusive and accessible." It has always been one of Apple's values, and they really want to encourage everyone to embrace it.

But it is important to remember that, mainly, accessibility is not about laws or even code. It is all about people, empathy, and good design for everyone.

Hopefully you already have enough reasons. I know you were convinced already when I just said it was the right thing to do. Or even when you started reading this book! But now you already have some powerful arguments for anyone that dares asking you not to spend time developing or testing apps for accessibility.

Accessibility and inclusion: What is the difference?

There is a distinction between accessibility and inclusion, although usually you'll work with both to create experiences that are usable and open to everyone.

Accessibility is both an attribute that defines the qualities that make an experience for everyone and the professional discipline aimed at achieving that goal. We don't want to build something that just works for the average user. We should offer a variety of ways for using our app so that everyone can participate in what we have created. We immediately think our users will use the screen of their devices as both input and output mechanisms to use our app. But that is not always the case. Users may use sound or haptic feedback to get information back from our app and voice or a keyboard to interact with it. Remember that when it comes to people, there is no such thing as normal, we all are different and have different abilities.

When talking about inclusion, we have to think not just about how to make technology accessible to people with very different backgrounds, age, gender, abilities, language, education, etc., but also to make them feel part of it once they have access. If you are using an app that gives you public transport options to get to different places in a city, even if the app itself is accessible, it may not be very inclusive if you don't have the possibility to know which train stations are adapted for wheelchair users or provide sound announcements, for example.

Accessibility lets people use apps, inclusion makes them belong.

Assistive technology

When thinking about assistive technologies, we can imagine our app as a content deliverer and the assistive technology as the technology, equipment, or product – provided in this case by Apple – that will allow our app to be accessed by the user in different ways depending on the user's needs. Some examples of assistive technologies are screen readers like VoiceOver, braille output systems, magnification, voice input and dictation, switch access... We all benefit from assistive technologies. We also use assistive technologies in the real world. Think about glasses, wheelchairs, or crutches... They are pieces of technology that help you interact with the world around you in a different way depending on your needs.

Who are your users?

We tend to think about disabilities in a very polarized way, and when developing, we mostly think about totally blind people. But there are many types of blindness. People may just have low vision – maybe caused by aging – or some might be color-blind, or sensitive to bright lights, etc.

In addition to vision challenges, your users may also face motor, hearing (deaf, hard of hearing...), or learning and cognitive challenges (dyslexia, autism...). You'll find that Apple often categorizes its accessibility features in those four groups, as you can see in Figure 1-2.

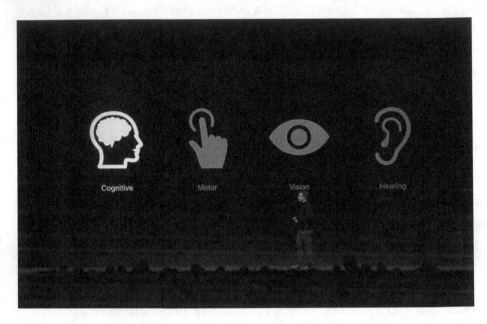

Figure 1-2. *Apple's four areas of focus for making technology accessible*

Someone might be permanently disabled, but disabilities can also be temporary or even situational. Microsoft defines "The Persona Spectrum," as you can see in Figure 1-3 from their great "Inclusive – Microsoft Design" guide (`www.microsoft.com/design/inclusive`). It really helps to open your mind about the diversity of impairments someone can face and also how it is not difficult at all for any of us to fall in one of those categories at any point in our lives.

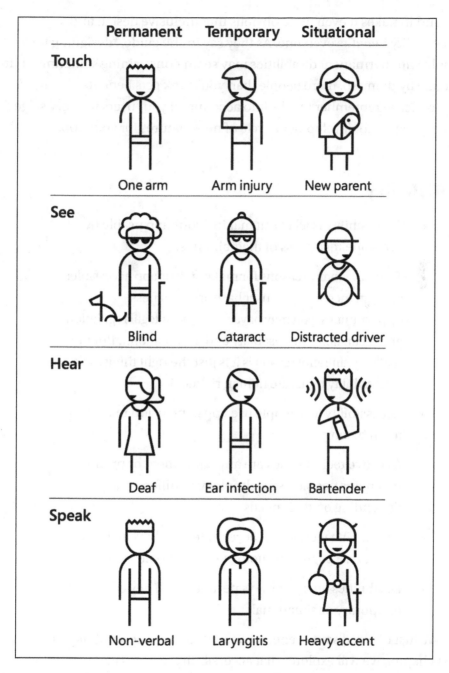

Figure 1-3. *The Persona Spectrum, Microsoft*

And it makes it even more obvious that inclusive design and accessibility benefits everyone. As they say in the guide, "designing for people with permanent disabilities may seem constraining sometimes but actually by doing so, more people than you think gets benefited."

So please remember to take into account all your users in every stage of the design and development cycle of new features for your app.

Summary

- Accessibility is all about making your app usable by everyone regardless of their abilities.

- There are many reasons for making your app accessible: you can increase your user base and business opportunities, you may have to consider legal regulations, and it can help with usability and automation... But the really meaningful reason is it is just the right thing to do. Accessibility rights are human rights.

- Accessibility lets people use apps, inclusion makes them belong.

- Assistive technologies are any equipment or product that helps people use technology in different ways depending on their needs.

- For making technology accessible, you have to think of four areas: cognitive, motor, vision, and hearing.

- Disabilities are not always permanent. They can also be temporary or situational.

We just covered some general concepts around accessibility. In the next chapter, we will explore what accessibility features and technologies iOS has to offer to its users.

CHAPTER 2

Accessibility features in iOS

It is time for an introduction to the different assistive technologies iOS has to offer and what their purpose is. We will have an overview of some of the features that the system provides, and that should work with your app out of the box, and we will have a deeper look into the ones that will require some more development work to create an appropriate and accessible experience. Figure 2-1, from one of the accessibility sessions at Apple's WWDC, is an example of the variety of technologies available provided by Apple, and it shows the importance that the company gives to accessibility.

© Daniel Devesa Derksen-Staats 2019
D. D. Derksen-Staats, *Developing Accessible iOS Apps*,
https://doi.org/10.1007/978-1-4842-5308-3_2

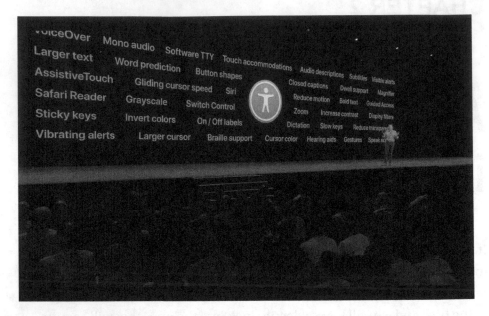

Figure 2-1. *Some of the accessibility technologies Apple offers*

Screen reader: VoiceOver

VoiceOver is a screen reader, but it does much more than that. It is
an alternative way of using iOS – and also macOS and pretty much
every Apple device – and, therefore, your apps. It uses gestures on
touch devices, a keyboard or even a braille display to give users equal
opportunity to access your app, and get feedback from it, independently
of their abilities.

Apple does a great job, so your apps are usable with VoiceOver with
a minimum effort from the app developers. But still, as they say, "Every
person who uses your app has access to VoiceOver. But not necessarily
every VoiceOver user has access to every app." And it is worth checking
that your apps are not among them.

We'll get hands-on with the code later, but first it is a good idea to get
familiarized with how you can turn on/off VoiceOver and learn some basic
gestures to use it in iOS.

Enabling VoiceOver

You can find and enable VoiceOver in Settings ➤ Accessibility ➤ VoiceOver (Figure 2-2). In iOS 13, the Accessibility settings was moved to the main Settings page. It was a great decision from Apple for giving it more visibility. So, if you are using a previous iOS version, VoiceOver is in Settings ➤ General ➤ Accessibility ➤ VoiceOver instead. They now even let the user configure some accessibility features in the Quick Start onboarding process too.

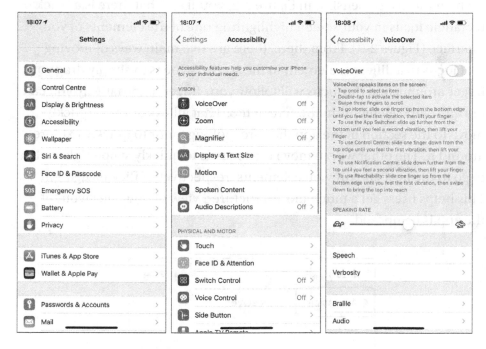

Figure 2-2. *Steps to find VoiceOver in Settings*

But before turning on VoiceOver, I recommend you two things. The first one is to learn the basics, so you don't get mad trying to find your way to turn it off again. Luckily it is pretty well explained in the Settings page (last screenshot in Figure 2-2), and we'll also have a look at the basic gestures in this chapter. Second, it is really handy to set a shortcut to enable/disable it easily. It will make your life easier, especially when you want to test your app or to see how Apple apps, or others, implement VoiceOver for certain use cases. We will see how to configure shortcuts in this chapter too.

How to use VoiceOver

As soon as you enable VoiceOver, by toggling the VoiceOver switch, as seen on the last screenshot in Figure 2-2, you'll see that there is a black rectangle focus in your screen highlighting one of the elements of your interface (Figure 2-3). From there, there are two main ways of moving that focus to a different element in the screen. One is to simply drag your finger around, and the focus will follow your finger; alternatively you can tap any of the elements in the screen too. That allows users to quickly move to the section of the app they are looking for or to quickly explore around it. The other way to move the focus is to quickly swipe right or left to go to the next and previous elements, respectively – flick navigation. This helps users get a much more structured view of how the layout of the app is composed.

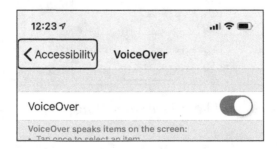

Figure 2-3. *VoiceOver settings screen when VoiceOver is turned on*

Because a tap will just move the focus to the desired UI element to describe that element to you, you'll need a double tap – anywhere on the screen – to interact with the focused element, in the case it is an interactive element such as a button, or a switch, etc.

If you need to disable VoiceOver again, just select the VoiceOver cell with the switch and double tap.

A few more gestures

Now you know the most basic gestures to interact with VoiceOver using a touch screen. But there is more. A three-finger swipe will let you scroll through scrollable content in a pagination mode.

And you may be a bit lost if suddenly you find yourself in the lock screen, Control Center, or the Notification Center, especially if your device doesn't have a home button. You just need to remember a couple more gestures for that: a swipe up from the bottom edge of the screen till the first vibration or sound brings you to Home. If you continue swiping up to the second vibration or sound, you will open the App Switcher. On the other hand, if you swipe down from the top edge of the screen till the first vibration or sound, you'll open Control Center. If you continue to the second vibration or sound, you will open the Notification Center. If you are not sure, wait a second before letting your finger go off the screen and VoiceOver will hint you with the action you are about to perform. I recommend this great video from Apple explaining all these VoiceOver navigation gestures: `https://youtu.be/qDm7GiKra28`.

At this point you can do pretty much everything with VoiceOver. There are some other power user features that are great to know when adapting your app for VoiceOver, and we will learn more about it in Chapters 3, 4 and 7.

Shortcuts

There are a few accessibility shortcuts that you can enable and that come quite handy when testing or for easy and quicker access if you need any of them. In the Accessibility settings, look for the Accessibility Shortcut option (Figure 2-4). Enable the options you want, and, from that moment, those options will be just a triple tap on the home button away – the side button if you don't have a home button. Or even better, you can customize your controls in Control Center to have a button for Accessibility Shortcut too.

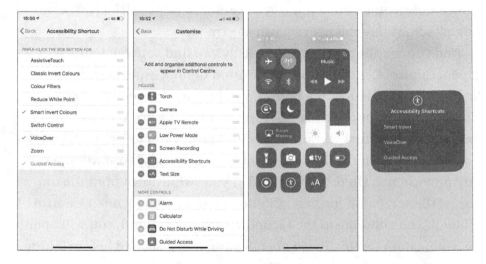

Figure 2-4. *Steps to add Accessibility Shortcut to Control Center*

Vision

VoiceOver is arguably the most popular assistive technology in iOS. It is the first option you find in the Accessibility settings and, as you can see, it is highly customizable. But it is not the only one. There are many other settings and customizations that can help people with a vision impairment.

Display and Text Size

It includes several features such as Auto-Brightnes, On/Off Labels, Color Filters (Grayscale, Red/Green Filter, etc.), Reduce White Point (for reducing the intensity of bright colors in the screen), etc. We'll further explore some other of these features in the chapter, like Bold Text, Smart Invert Colors, Button Shapes, or Reduce Transparency. These UI customizations may require some support from your app to work properly.

Bold Text

It allows users to have a UI with a bolder font that can be easier to read (Figure 2-5). Like many things in accessibility, this feature comes for free if you are using the system font or, even better, a text style. If you are manually setting a different font, like Helvetica, or using a custom font, you'll need to do some work to support this feature. But don't worry, we'll show you how.

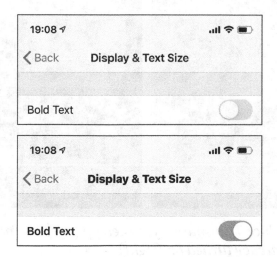

Figure 2-5. *Bold Text turned off (top) compared to Bold Text turned on (bottom)*

Reduce Transparency

Transparency may reduce the color contrast ratio of some text, icons, etc., with the background, which might be an issue for some users (Figure 2-6). This will automatically work with native components like *UITabBar* or *UINavigationBar*, but it will need a couple lines of code to be supported if you have a custom UI component with transparency.

Figure 2-6. *Reduce Transparency turned off (left) compared to Reduce Transparency turned on (right)*

Invert Colors

It inverts the colors of the screen, so everything is mostly displayed with light text over dark backgrounds, as opposed to the habitual light backgrounds with dark text. The problem is that it inverts everything, including images, videos, etc. That is why Apple introduced Smart Invert Colors in iOS 11, allowing developers to provide a much better experience by opting out some UI elements from being inverted.

These UI customizations will just work. They won't require any support from the developer.

Button Shapes

Buttons, since iOS 7, are defined by the tint color of the app. If you are perhaps color-blind, you may have issues distinguishing them. This option will also underline them so they're easier to find. The tab bar also shows you the selected tab using color; this option also helps with this issue by shadowing the selected tab. As we'll see, signaling something in just one way, like color, tends not to be very accessible, but this gives you a workaround for the buttons use case.

Zoom

It does exactly what the name describes; it magnifies the screen if the user needs to zoom in a region to be able to see any details a bit closer. It has a few customizations about zoom level and also different ways of controlling it to adapt it to your needs, like zooming in the whole screen or just a small fraction of it.

Magnifier

It allows the user to have a quick access to the camera with a zoom, so you can use it to magnify anything around you.

Physical and motor

There are many tools in iOS to help users that might have motor impairments (cerebral palsy, muscular dystrophy, ALS, etc.).

Assistive Touch

Assistive Touch is one of the most important ones. It allows the user to customize a menu on the screen to access, with a single tap, functions of the system that may require special gestures, such as swiping down to get the notifications panel, a double tap, or even more complex ones like 3D touch (Figure 2-7). Assistive Touch is great for users that find specific gestures too difficult to perform or that require an adaptive accessory. It even allows you to configure custom gestures. You may have seen people using this menu when their home button was broken.

In iPadOS it also lets you use a pointing device like a Bluetooth mouse, trackpad, or even a joystick to control your iPad.

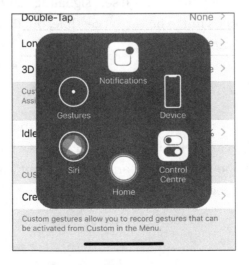

Figure 2-7. *Example of Assistive Touch menu*

Switch Control

Switch Control is also a very important feature in iOS for people with limited mobility. It allows you to use your iOS device with one or multiple physical buttons or switches. It sequentially highlights items on the screen that can be activated with one of the configured switches through an adaptive accessory or keyboard. It is incredible how users can manage to perform really complicated tasks like editing video with Switch Control.

Voice Control

New in iOS 13, Apple presented Voice Control at the WWDC 2019, and I think it was actually one of the coolest features presented. It allows you to control the entire system just with your voice.

Before iOS 13 you could control certain functions of your phone using Siri, but it has two big limitations: the first one is that the device needs to be connected to the Internet, and the second one is that it has very limited functionality and it relies on developers implementing Siri Intents or Shortcuts with *SiriKit*. Voice Control removes these two limitations. It can be used offline, and it is a more general tool that allows you to navigate the system by a series of commands. It relies on *UIAccessibility*, so it is still important to take it into account when, for example, setting up your accessibility labels to your UI components, as we will see in the next chapter.

There are a ton of commands. These are some of the things you can do with Voice Control:

- Some are for basic navigation like Open Spotlight or Go Home, etc.

- Basic gestures including Scroll Down, Swipe Left, or Zoom In. And more advanced gestures like Drag and Drop or Tap and Hold.

- You can dictate, navigate, select, edit, and delete text.

- Control device-based configurations like changing the volume, or completely muting the sound, rotating the screen, or locking the device.

But one of the smartest features is the possibility to use a series of overlays to control the device. You can show a grid with numbers over the screen or see labels with numbers or names (based on accessibility labels) over the elements in the screen that can be interacted with, as you can see in Figure 2-8. It is totally worth giving it a try and having a look around all the possible commands in Settings. It works almost like magic. A good trick is to ask Voice Control to show the labels when using your app. It is a great way to visualize the accessibility labels you have configured, and it helps you identify labels that can have been set incorrectly or that can be improved.

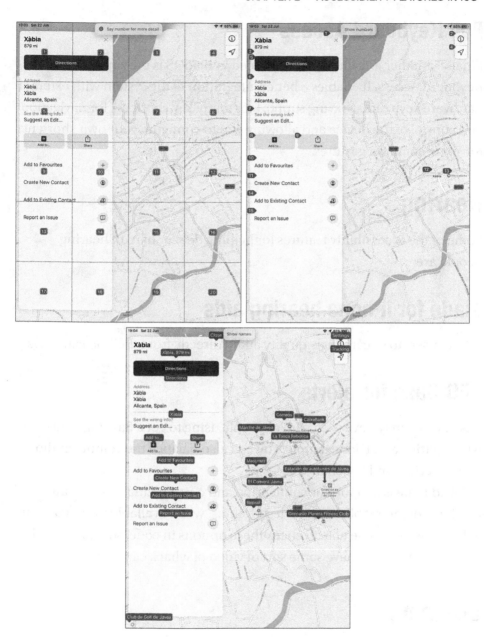

Figure 2-8. *Navigation modes with Voice Control*

Full Keyboard Access

Finally, another great feature introduced in iPadOS is the support for Full Keyboard Access. It enables a better integration of the system with external hardware keyboards, having support for many key shortcuts for navigation and control of the device and allowing you to configure your own shortcuts for some common gestures.

Hearing

Some of the accessibility features for helping deaf or hard of hearing people are:

Made for iPhone hearing aids

Allows users to stream high-quality audio directly from their hearing aids.

LED flash for alerts

It is one you may have seen a lot of people using to get a flashing light when getting a call, for example; you can also balance the volume audio between right and left channels.

And there is support for configuring and customizing subtitles and captions, or for enabling audio descriptions, when available, by default. As a developer, you'll be able to check these options in code, so it plays well with your app if you have some sort of video playback capabilities.

Learning

Guided Access is the main feature provided by the system for users with learning needs.

Guided Access

It forces the device to stay in a single app, and it allows you to define which areas of the screen you can interact with. There is also the possibility to configure time limits.

Summary

- VoiceOver is Apple's screen reader pre-installed in iOS.

- Before enabling VoiceOver, it is a good idea to learn how to perform some basic gestures and how to switch it off.

- Configuring accessibility shortcuts will help you turn on/off quickly and will come handy for easily testing your app.

- Apple has accessibility features for covering the four areas we mentioned in the previous chapter: vision, motor, hearing, and cognitive.

Now that we are more familiar with a wide range of accessibility features included in iOS, it is time to get hands-on with the code. In the next chapter, we will learn how to make your app play nicely with VoiceOver.

CHAPTER 3

VoiceOver 101 – The fundamentals

In this chapter we will start to deep dive into the accessibility APIs offered by Apple, especially *UIAccessibility*. We will learn that by using native *UIKit* components, your app can be accessible with very little effort. We will also go through some of the best practices to create a great experience for VoiceOver users, including how to label your UI components properly, what is the Rotor, and a grand tour of the most important accessibility traits and how to implement them appropriately.

Understanding UIAccessibility

It is time to have a look at some code. You'll find all the code examples from this book in this repo: `https://github.com/Apress/developing-accessible-iOS-apps`. At the core of accessibility in *UIKit*, we have *UIAccessibility*. From Apple's documentation it can be defined as "a set of methods that provide accessibility information about views and controls in an app's user interface." Assistive technologies like VoiceOver, Voice Control, or Switch Control will rely on the correct implementation of these APIs to help users interact with your app with their preferred input/output mechanisms (screen reader, braille keyboard, switches, voice, etc.) depending on their needs.

© Daniel Devesa Derksen-Staats 2019
D. D. Derksen-Staats, *Developing Accessible iOS Apps*,
https://doi.org/10.1007/978-1-4842-5308-3_3

The following code shows an example of some of the most common accessibility properties in *UIAccessibility*:

```
// Do I serve a purpose?
accessibleView.isAccessibilityElement = true

// What is my name?
accessibleView.accessibilityLabel = NSLocalizedString
("accessibility.close_button", comment: "")

// What is my personality?
accessibleView.accessibilityTraits = UIAccessibilityTraitButton

// What is my value?
accessibleView.accessibilityValue = NSLocalizedString
("accessibility.selector_value", comment: "")

// Where am I?
accessibleView.accessibilityFrame = UIAccessibilityConvertFrame
ToScreenCoordinates(accessibleView.frame, view)
```

You can see it as five essential questions for defining a UI component as accessible:

- **isAccessibilityElement**: Most UI controls have this value set to *true* by default. *UIView*s don't. So if you are defining custom controls, you may find that you have to set this property to *true* if you want VoiceOver to find it.

- **accessibilityLabel**: For native UI controls, it is inferred from the control title. It is what VoiceOver will announce first. It is a good idea to localize the label so that it works in any language you support.

- ***accessibilityTraits***: They can be combined with the "|" operator. They are also combined with the ones in the superclass too. Examples of different traits are Adjustable, Selected, Not Enabled… They are localized for you. Traits are very important, because they define the context around the UI component. We'll come back to them later.

- ***accessibilityValue***: Read by VoiceOver when it differs from the label. Some examples are a slider value or a text field that could have a label like "Name", but the value would be the text entered.

- ***accessibilityFrame***: Already set for any *UIView* and subclasses. It defines where the UI element is in the screen coordinate system.

Some of these properties can be configured from the Identity Inspector in the Interface Builder when selecting an element, but most of the examples in the book will show how to deal with them in code. There is nothing wrong with configuring things in Interface Builder, but doing it in code has some benefits like the ability to localize the accessibility labels you want to use or tweak the behavior based on the user's interactions.

And there are many other properties. We'll explore some of them in the following chapters.

Accessibility labels

Getting your accessibility labels right is probably one of the most important things you have to do to offer a great experience for your VoiceOver users. In principle, the label will be the title of the component, if it has one. If it hasn't, setting an accessibility label is just a matter of assigning a meaningful string to the UI component's accessibility label property. It is better if you set a localized string, that way it will work for all the languages your app supports.

Buttons

One case in which it is easy to forget setting an accessibility label is when creating a button that has an icon image but not a title. If we don't set it, VoiceOver will just read the name of the image you used. If you named the file sensibly, you may be lucky, but chances are the names of your images are full of abbreviations and naming conventions that you have with your designers that wouldn't be good accessibility labels, like "close_icon_64px_ blue@3x". Furthermore, the name of a file is not localized. Think about that settings cog button item in your navigation bar, the "X" button for closing your modal view, or any playback control buttons, etc. All those examples are good places to go and check that you didn't forget to add an accessibility label that makes sense.

```
// Setting an accessibility label with a localized string
button.accessibilityLabel = NSLocalizedString("accessibility.
close_button", comment: "")
```

It is also important to keep it as short as possible; we don't want to create experiences that are too verbose. But there are some cases in which a bit more context is needed. For example, a good label for a button with a "+" icon could be just "Add." That would be enough in some situations. If it is placed in the navigation bar, for example, it is probably representing a global action in that section of the app where the context is clear. Could it be adding a new note? Or creating a new photo album? But if it is within the content of the app, it may require further clarification. Consider a music app example: is it clear that you are adding the album to your music library? Or are you adding a song to a playlist? Or are you following an artist in which case "Follow" would be a better label? If it is not clear, you may want to add some more information in the accessibility label, like "Add song." If it is still not clear, you can also use a hint for further explanation on what actioning the button does. We will talk about hints later in the chapter.

We also want to avoid redundancy. Back to the music app example, if we are in the player, we also know we are dealing with a song. Instead of "Play song," "Pause song," "Skip song," "Repeat song,"... we can just use "Play," "Pause," "Skip," or "Repeat."

Some buttons also change their state and mean different things. In that case we want to remember to update the label when the state changes. If we have a follow button, when pressed, it may change to an unfollow button. Or a button for adding a song to a playlist may change to delete from the playlist, once added.

And finally, when adding accessibility labels, please never add the type of the element to the label, as VoiceOver will already vocalize the traits of the component. More on accessibility traits later in the chapter too. This is something that happens a lot in the case of buttons. It wouldn't be a good practice to use the word "button" in the accessibility label. If we added the label "Add button" in the previous example, VoiceOver would read "Add button. Button" and that would just be unnecessary duplicated information.

In short, I would say that, when setting our accessibility labels, we want to give as much context as possible avoiding verbosity and redundancy.

Abbreviations

Sometimes you will also need to set a different accessibility label to the title of the UI component. A classic example is when showing times like 01:30 for minutes and seconds or when using abbreviations like 2d for 2 days or 2 days ago, although sometimes VoiceOver is smart enough to read properly some date abbreviations.

The following code shows an example of how you could create an accessibility label that reads durations in minutes and seconds in a natural way:

```
// Formatting the time in a readable format
let dateComponentsFormatter = DateComponentsFormatter()
let timeFormatter = DateFormatter()
```

```
timeFormatter.dateFormat = "mm:ss"
dateComponentsFormatter.allowedUnits = [.minute, .second]
dateComponentsFormatter.unitStyle = .full

if let date = timeFormatter.date(from: time) {
        let components = Calendar.current.dateComponents
        ([.minute, .second], from:date)
        durationLabel.accessibilityLabel = dateComponents
        Formatter.string(from: components)
}
```

Pro tip   When dealing with units or information that needs formatting (currency, time, and dates, or even addresses, etc.), you will almost always find some formatter in Foundation that will help you deal with them, especially if you need to internationalize or localize them, and you will also have a higher chance of VoiceOver reading them properly.

Remember to test it

And some other times you will find that VoiceOver might read something in a way you were not expecting, so it is important to test your app and find those scenarios. For example, sometimes in English a word might be written exactly the same way but read differently depending on the context. These are a couple examples where you might want to set special accessibility labels:

```
// Live Video
"accessibilitylabel.live" = "Lyve";
// Most Read
"accessibilitylabel.mostread" = "Most Red";
```

Another case in which VoiceOver may read things in a different way than the one you would expect is with words that are in a different language. Take the word "Paella" (typical rice dish from Valencia, Spain), for example. One solution can be to define accessibility-attributed labels. One of the attributes lets you specify the language VoiceOver should use to read that label.

```
// Specifying the language for an accessibility label
recipeLabel.accessibilityAttributedLabel = NSAttributed
String(string: "Paella", attributes: [.accessibility
SpeechLanguage: "es-ES"])
```

Or, for further control, if you need to, you could specify the IPA (International Phonetic Alphabet) notation. For that, you just need to configure your text with an attributed string for a defined range and add an *.accessibilitySpeechIPANotation* as the key and the IPA notation as its value. And if that word is within a phrase – like with any other attributed string – you can specify the attributes just for a specific range.

```
// Specifying the language for a word in an accessibility label
let ipaAttributedText = NSMutableAttributedString(string:
"Paella is a Valencian rice dish")
let ipaRange = ipaAttributedText.string.range(of: "Paella")!
ipaAttributedText.addAttributes([.accessibilitySpeech
IPANotation: "pa'eʎa"], range: NSRange(ipaRange, in:
ipaAttributedText.string))
ipaLabel.attributedText = ipaAttributedText
```

And finally, another accessibility-attributed label property you can use is *.accessibilitySpeechPunctuation*, which indicates that VoiceOver should vocalize the punctuation marks.

```
// VoiceOver to vocalize punctuation marks
label.accessibilityAttributedLabel = NSAttributedString
(string: "Text within ' and ' or \" denote either speech or a
quotation", attributes: [.accessibilitySpeechPunctuation: true])
```

But there are many other tweaks and configurations available. So, if when testing VoiceOver anything sounds odd, you may find something in the attributed strings documentation for accessibility attributes that helps you create a more natural experience with VoiceOver: `https://developer.apple.com/documentation/uikit/accessibility/uiaccessibility/speech_attributes_for_attributed_strings`

And one more thing…, or two

Animations and spinners: it is quite easy to forget to configure a label for your animations that are communicating important information, for example, when "Loading…," "Updating…," or "Uploading…" any content in your app. Please give your spinner a label. I know most of times your app loads really fast, but sometimes users might have poor signal and it can take a couple seconds.

The verbosity exception rule: I know I said we must avoid verbosity, but sometimes in order to give enough context, you may need to be verbose. This may happen with information that is very visual. If there are photos, it is great to properly give some details about the images. Or with a stickers pack app, where it is great to explain what each sticker is about. It is all about finding the right balance: avoid unnecessary verbosity while providing information that is useful.

Accessibility traits

Traits give assistive technologies extra information on how to treat a UI component and what the user can do with it. There are many – around 17 at the time of writing this book – and it is better to understand what they are for with some examples:

Header

Some traits make navigation much easier. Imagine having to read this book without any headings at all. Think about how useful it is to be able to quickly visually identify the different chapters and sections in the book to find the information you need straight away or to pick it up where you left it before. There is a way of letting VoiceOver users jump from one section to the next/previous one, and, for that, we'll need to introduce the concept of the Rotor first.

You can use the Rotor (Figure 3-1) and select one of its options by using two fingers and rotating them on the screen around a center point, as if you were using an invisible knob. And as you rotate, it will speak all the options you can use to navigate the app. Once you select the Headings option, for example, you can navigate using swipes up/down to go to the previous/next header.

One of the options is "Headings." So if you select to navigate by headings in the Rotor, you can swipe down to go to the next heading or up to go to the previous one.

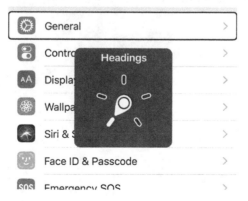

Figure 3-1. *The Rotor*

Finally, in the VoiceOver settings, you can customize the options in the Rotor. There are tons of them (speaking character by character/word by word..., changing the speaking rate, changing the typing mode, etc.), and it is worth going through the list to check that your app supports them correctly.

For VoiceOver to know that your UI element represents a heading, you just need to use the header trait.

```
// Configuring an accessibility trait as a header
headingLabel.accessibilityTraits = UIAccessibilityTraits.header
```

This is quite common when you need to group some content in an app in different subsections in one view controller, for example, when you have headers in a table view or collection view. The screenshots (Figure 3-2) are two good examples. The first one is from the Search screen in the BBC News app. Just imagine how many swipes you would need to get to the "More Topics" section if those headings didn't have the right header trait configured. The second example is from the Settings screen in the BBC+ app. It would be difficult to mentally structure and group all the settings options in the different categories if they weren't organized in subsections with their corresponding heading.

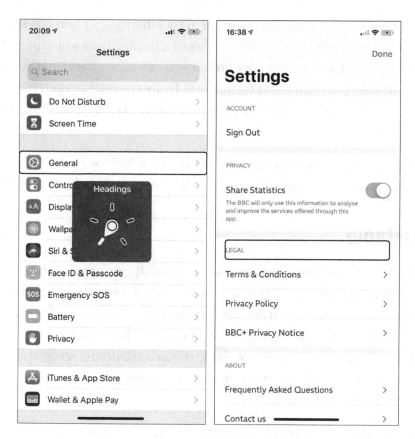

Figure 3-2. BBC News (left) and BBC+ (right) examples

Button

You will also find that sometimes you need to configure a specific accessibility trait when you are trying to write a custom component that will mimic a native counterpart. For example, you may want to write a custom button because you want it to have a nice animation when the user taps on it.

You may start creating this component by inheriting a plain *UIView*. When the user brings the VoiceOver focus to a button, they will expect it to vocalize the label followed by "button", so you can understand that you can interact with it. That important context will be lost in your custom button. Luckily, as you can see in the code, it is really easy to fix by just setting the button trait.

```
// Configuring an accessibility trait as a button
animatedButton.accessibilityTraits = UIAccessibilityTraits.button
```

Adjustable

It might be quite rare that you create adjustable UI components, but it is not strange at all to use *UISliders*. *UISliders* are accessible by default, they have the adjustable trait and an accessibility value that gets updated and that can be adjusted by swiping up or down. When you have an adjustable component, you can override the *accessibilityIncrement()* and *accessibilityDecrement()* functions to adjust the component to values that make sense when using VoiceOver.

```
// Configuring an accessibility trait as a button
override func accessibilityIncrement() {
        value += stepSize
        accessibilityValue = readableValue()
        sendActions(for: .valueChanged)
}

override func accessibilityDecrement() {
        value -= stepSize
        accessibilityValue = readableValue()
        sendActions(for: .valueChanged)
}
```

For example, if your slider shows prices from $100,000 to $2,000,000, you might want to increment and decrement in chunks of $100,000 - which would be the value of the variable *stepSize* in the code -, and not of $1 or $10, or it would be almost impossible to adjust it to sensible values.

You may also want to send a value-changed action just in case you are relying on that action for some other logic, like updating the text of a label so that it reflects the value of the slider.

Don't worry about the accessibility value for the moment, we'll get to it in the next section, in which we'll also see an example of a possible implementation for the *readableValue()* function.

The important thing to remember here is that this is the way you can allow a user to adjust your adjustable UI component and to decide which value to set the component to when it gets incremented/decremented.

Some other examples of adjustable components you may have in your app can be carousels for picking up an item or custom components for rating like the one in the image (Figure 3-3), which is included in the code examples repository of the book.

Figure 3-3. *Example of a rating UI component*

And more

The best thing you can do is to go to Apple's documentation and familiarize yourself with some of the traits available (link, selected, not available, etc.) and come back to them especially when you are creating custom UI components or navigation patterns in your app: `https://developer.apple.com/documentation/uikit/accessibility/uiaccessibility/accessibility_traits`.

Accessibility value

Imagine that you are developing a UI component that needs to hold a value. The classic examples are a progress bar for playback content, or a volume slider, or a text field whose value depends on the text that the user types. So if you are implementing a UI component instead of using a *UISlider* or *UITextField*, or any other custom component that holds a value, you will have to configure this property accordingly.

But as we've seen with the native *UISlider*, despite being accessible by default, it might need some tweaks. The default format for its value is a percentage. As in this example from Apple Music: "Volume, 62%". But percentages are not always a helpful format. If you are listening to a song, you probably want to know the exact minutes and seconds of the progress instead of knowing the percentage of the song you've heard. Or if the slider represents prices like in the previous example, you want VoiceOver to vocalize exactly the selected price. If it goes from 1 to 10 dollars and the slider is right in the middle, "5 dollars" will be much more useful information than "50%". The accessibility value is a string and as you can see in the code example, number formatters might again help you in this case for setting up a readable value.

```
// Configuring the accessibility value with a currency
let sliderValueString = NumberFormatter.localizedString
(from: NSNumber(value: slider.value), number: .currency)
slider.accessibilityValue = sliderValueString
```

Accessibility hints

They are optional. It is very useful when a UI component needs further explanation on what it does or how to interact with it. They need to be carefully used as they can make VoiceOver very verbose. The good news is that they will be read after a pause, always after the label and the corresponding trait, value, etc. This way, any experienced user that knows already how to use the app can skip this information and carry on using the app. It is a good practice to start it with a verb, as you are going to describe what it does or how to use it. Some examples taken from the Apple Music app too are:

- "Double tap and hold, wait for the sound, then drag to rearrange." This is what VoiceOver vocalizes when moving the focus to the draggable control for rearranging songs in a playlist.

- "Double tap to expand the mini player." When playing a song, you can minimize the fullscreen player, but a mini player will stick to the tab bar at the bottom of the screen, so you can see what is playing at all times. It is not immediately obvious that you can go back to the fullscreen player by double tapping it, so a hint in this case helps to learn how to better use the app.

```
// Configuring an accessibility hint for a UI control
draggableView.accessibilityHint = NSLocalizedString
("accessibility.draggable_hint", comment: "")
```

It is a good idea to localize the hint, so you can easily translate the app into different languages and give VoiceOver a hint in the user's preferred language.

Accessibility element

It is very tempting to start assigning the *isAccessbilityElement* property to *true* for every single view, but that doesn't always help and there is a reason why it is *false* by default in views and why you can even change it in any other *UIKit* component, where it is *true* by default, to *false*. Not every single element on the screen needs to be an accessibility element, and the only way to determine which ones do make sense to be set as accessible and which don't is by using and testing your app.

Take the price slider as an example again (Figure 3-4). If configured properly and a label and value are set, when VoiceOver has its focus on the slider component, it should vocalize something like: "Price. Four hundred and fifty thousand pounds. Adjustable. Swipe up or down with one finger to adjust the value." That is all the information the user needs. The labels with the text "Price:" and "£450,000.00" have redundant information for VoiceOver, and it could be a better experience to set them as not accessible elements. Images that are purely decorative and that don't convey relevant information don't need to be accessible elements either.

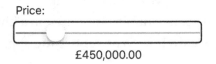

Figure 3-4. *Interacting with a slider with VoiceOver*

The joy of using UIKit components

One thing you quickly learn when you start doing some iOS development is that using native *UIKit* components as much as possible is going to make your life immensely easier. This is due to the fact that when Apple introduces new features or improvements in the SDK, you'll get most of those for free or with very little implementation effort. Some examples are when Apple introduced split screen in the iPad, drag and drop, peek and pop, devices with new screen shapes like the iPhone X, right-to-left support in iOS…, and many others. All those features were very easy to adopt if you were using size classes, *UITableView* and *UICollectionView*,

UINavigationController and *UITabBarController*, etc. But it could easily become weeks or even months of development work if your app was using custom implementations.

That can also be the case for accessibility. By using native *UIKit* components, your app will be much more accessible than you might be even expecting, because the framework does the heavy-lifting work for you. The controls will have the right traits for VoiceOver and these will be localized, the accessibility labels will be inferred from the title of the component, navigation gestures will work as expected, etc.

But when developers opt for developing custom UI controls, they very often forget about addressing any accessibility issues that these components might have. It is totally fine to develop your own UI component if you need it to support any functionality that shall not be present in its native version. However, it is important to remember to set the appropriate accessibility properties. It is also important to know that users are accustomed to the standard behavior from the apps that come pre-installed in iOS. That is why it can be a good idea to try for it to behave as much as possible as its Apple's counterpart, so that the user knows what to expect when navigating your app.

For example, when creating custom tab bars, developers sometimes forget to implement the right accessibility properties and functionality. When using VoiceOver on a tab bar, using Apple Music's example, it will read something like "Selected. Library, tab. One of five." If you swipe right, it will go to the next tab, and you'll hear something like "For You. Tab. Two of five." You'd be surprised how often, when using an app with an in-house developed tab bar component, you get a very poor experience. I've seen multiple times apps that, when using VoiceOver, you just hear "Button" for each one of the tabs, especially if the tabs don't have a label with a title, and even if they do, it doesn't say important information like if the tab is selected or how many of them there are. Or even worse, sometimes they're not accessible at all if the developers haven't even used *UIButton*s in the implementation.

If I could give any advice to new iOS developers when they start, that would probably be basically to stick as much as possible with *UIKit* components to build your UI. As I said, not only will it make your app much more maintainable in the future, but it will also help you create more accessible apps.

Summary

- Accessibility labels have to give as much context as possible, avoiding verbosity and redundancy.

- Accessibility labels can be attributed. These attributes can specify the language of the label and even the IPA notation for further control on how the label should be vocalized by VoiceOver.

- The correct use of the Heading accessibility trait makes navigating with VoiceOver much easier and structured.

- Accessibility hints give users further explanation on how to interact with a UI component, but they are read after a pause so experienced users can skip them.

We have just learned some of the most important concepts for creating an app that works great with VoiceOver. But there is more; in the next chapter, we will bring the levels of support of your app with VoiceOver up to 11.

CHAPTER 4

VoiceOver – Up to 11

Now we know the foundations for creating accessible apps for VoiceOver users and even Voice Control users. But we don't want to stop there, we don't want our apps to be just usable, we want to go one step further and make them exceptional and delightful, for all our users. Let's bring our VoiceOver support to the next level.

Did you know that a Magic Tap – double tap with two fingers – should execute the main action of the current view? Or that a "Z" gesture with two fingers means Perform Escape and should close the current view? In this chapter we'll tune your VoiceOver skills up to 11.

ACCESSIBILITY

Figure 4-1. *Accessibility* ➤ *Up to 11*

Advanced VoiceOver gestures

These custom actions are less known by non-VoiceOver users, but if you want to go beyond offering an acceptable experience and offer an excellent one instead, this is a good place to start by implementing both the Performe Escape action and Magic Tap where it makes sense.

© Daniel Devesa Derksen-Staats 2019
D. D. Derksen-Staats, *Developing Accessible iOS Apps*,
https://doi.org/10.1007/978-1-4842-5308-3_4

Perform Escape

This is one of the most useful VoiceOver actions that developers forget to implement. But imagine for one second that, when presenting a view controller in a navigation controller, the back button was not there or didn't respond. Or that a modal view was presented with a tiny close or done button that had a very small hit area, so it made the view very difficult to dismiss. You would consider all those serious bugs and you would probably get frustrated with the app and stop using it, or in the case that it was your own app, you would probably prioritize some bug tickets to be able to fix them in the next release.

This is exactly the kind of experience you might be offering to your VoiceOver users if you are not implementing the Perform Escape action. The Perform Escape action allows VoiceOver users to go back or get out of a section of your app with a two-finger scrub back and forth gesture – like drawing a "Z" on the screen.

If you are using a navigation controller, this gesture should already work for you out of the box. But if you are presenting view controllers with a custom mechanism or implementation, you may want to test it and make sure it works. It is a good idea to check any modal presentation too, including modal view controllers, popovers, custom alerts, custom action sheets, etc.

The good news again is that the implementation is really easy. You will just need to override the *accessibilityPerformEscape()* method to capture that gesture in the view or view controller and dismiss it appropriately. In the case of a modal view controller, it would be as easy as this:

```
// Dismiss modal view with an escape gesture when using VoiceOver
override func accessibilityPerformEscape() -> Bool {
    self.dismiss(animated: true, completion: nil)
    return true
}
```

Magic Tap

There are also lots of situations where there is a main action in a particular section of your app. That action is probably very well defined, maybe the button that triggers it is bigger, it has a predominant position in the UI, etc. It is easy to find and action.

Some examples would be a start/stop action in a timer app, the button to take a picture in a photography app, a player button in a music or video on demand app, etc.

Now imagine that you open the player and the play icon is somewhere you wouldn't expect like the top left corner, or that it is very small or not noticeable at all. That would be strange as it is probably the button that all your users are going to look for as soon as they open the app.

This is a similar example as the Perform Escape action; it is called Magic Tap. A VoiceOver user will expect that main action to be triggered when performing a double tap with two fingers on the screen. For example, double tap with two fingers to play and repeat the action to pause. In this case we just need to override the *accessibilityPerformMagicTap()* function. The code would look something similar to this:

```
// Perform play/pause actions with Magic Tap
override func accessibilityPerformMagicTap() -> Bool {
        if player.isPlaying {
                player.pause()
        } else {
                player.play()
        }
        return true
}
```

Managing the accessibility focus

Most of times you'll find that VoiceOver's focus goes where you would expect. If you swipe right, it moves to the next element; if you swipe left, it goes to the previous one. However, sometimes the UI changes as the user interacts with the app, and it is important to tell the accessibility framework how to behave in those situations. Again, this is something you will find more often when developing custom UI components. It will be easier to understand with some examples.

Is the accessibility view a modal view?

Imagine that you have to implement a little pop-up, maybe to show some more detailed information. Something like the one in the screenshot (Figure 4-2). You would find that VoiceOver can still "see" the UI elements that are covered by the custom pop-up, and it creates a very confusing experience. This happens a lot when implementing things like slide-over hamburger menus, where VoiceOver starts jumping in a way that feels random between elements of the menu and the main content.

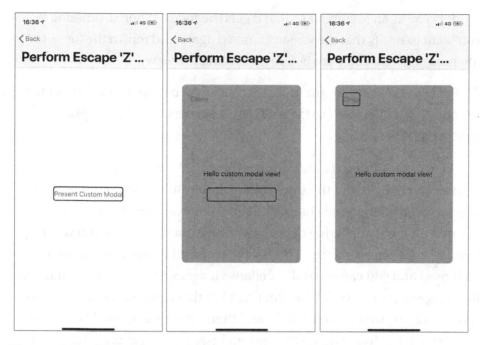

Figure 4-2. *Before presenting a custom modal view with VoiceOver (left). Incorrect implementation (center). Expected result (right)*

Fortunately, the accessibility framework has a property to define that a view should behave as a modal, "hiding" to VoiceOver any accessible elements that are siblings of the currently one on focus.

```
// Specify that a view behaves as a modal view
customModalView.accessibilityViewIsModal = true
```

Post notifications

Following previous example, when presenting the "modal" view, you would like the focus to move to the newly presented view, instead of staying in the button that has just been actioned. When major UI changes happen on screen, you may need to notify it. In this case, you would probably want to notify that the screen changed and pass the custom

51

modal view as an argument so that it gets the focus. When dismissing it, you want to notify that the screen changed again and return the focus to the button where you were before presenting the view.

```
// Post notification for a screen change on modal presentation
UIAccessibility.post(notification: .screenChanged, argument:
customModalView)
```

The *.screenChanged* notification is then used when a major portion of the screen changes, but there are some other notifications you may want to post when your screen changes slightly. For example, if what changes is a new element appearing or disappearing from the screen, you would use *.layoutChanged* instead. This is very useful when an information is collapsed and you can expand it, collapse it again, etc. Like the example in the image (Figure 4-3). On the other hand, if that element that appeared on screen is going to stay there briefly and then disappear again, like custom toast/snack bar-like component, custom in-app notifications, etc., you can use an *.announcement* notification instead.

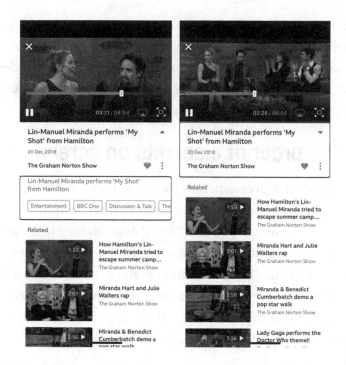

Figure 4-3. *Example of VoiceOver usage when some information in the screen has been hidden and a "Layout Changed" notification is sent*

Accessibility labels can be attributed labels, as we have seen before. And one of the attributes available lets you specify if an announcement should be queued or if it is important enough to interrupt any ongoing ones.

```
// Send a queued announcement
let queueAnnouncementAttributes = [NSAttributedString.Key.
accessibilitySpeechQueueAnnouncement: true]

let announcementAttributedString = NSAttributedString(string:
customToastView.accessibilityLabel!, attributes: queue
AnnouncementAttributes)

UIAccessibility.post(notification: .announcement, argument:
announcementAttributedString)
```

53

Another important notification you may want to post is when scrolling a view on behalf of the user: *.pageScrolled*.

If you would like to know more about it, you can find all the details in Apple's documentation: `https://developer.apple.com/documentation/uikit/uiaccessibility/notification`.

Control the order of elements on screen

As we have seen, VoiceOver generally moves its focus to the next element, going from left to right and from top to bottom, when swiping right. However, sometimes we tend to distribute things visually in a way that makes this default behavior not the best one for our UI to make sense when vocalized by VoiceOver. A common pattern in lots of apps, for example, is to place some key information in columns. Each column may have a title label and another label with the value of that info. Something like the example in the screenshot (Figure 4-4). Sounds familiar? I'm sure you have seen it a ton of times.

Figure 4-4. *Example of a profile-like UI*

In this case, VoiceOver will naturally move from the user's name to "Followers," then "Following," "Posts," "550," "340," and "750" (Figure 4-5). As you can see, that doesn't make much sense. "Followers" and "550" are two labels that work as one piece of information, and the same applies to "Following" with "340" and "Posts" with "750."

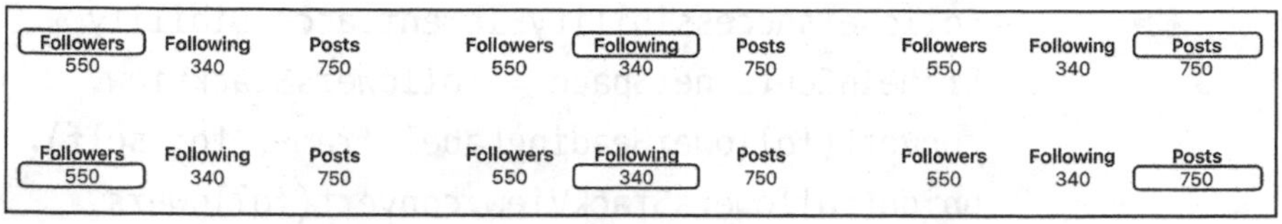

Figure 4-5. *Sequence of the default behavior when navigating the UI in Figure 4-4 using VoiceOver*

Fortunately, there are ways to fix this. Views can define their own accessibility elements as an array, and the order will follow the order in how the elements are placed in the array.

If we consider a view like the one in the image (Figure 4-4), which could be built with *UIStackView*s, the code could look something like the following code snippet, in which we define each one of the blocks of information as a single accessibility element. To achieve this, we can combine both labels and even change the accessibility frame to be the union of both labels too. Then we place them in the order we want and return them as the new array of accessibility elements for the view:

```
// Define a new array of accessibility elements
override var accessibilityElements: [Any]? {
        set {}
        get {
                var elements = [UIAccessibilityElement]()
                let followersAccessibilityElement = UI
                AccessibilityElement(accessibilityContainer: self)
                let followingAccessibilityElement = UI
                AccessibilityElement(accessibilityContainer: self)
                let postsAccessibilityElement = UIAccessibility
                Element(accessibilityContainer: self)

                followersAccessibilityElement.accessibility
                Label = "\(followerHeadingLabel.accessibility
                Label!), \(followersNumberLabel.accessibility
                Label!)"
```

55

```
        followersAccessibilityElement.accessibility
        FrameInContainerSpace = followersStackView.
        convert(followerHeadingLabel.frame, to: self).
        union(followersStackView.convert(followers
        NumberLabel.frame, to: self))
        elements.append(followersAccessibilityElement)

        followingAccessibilityElement.accessibility
        Label = "\(followingHeadingLabel.accessibility
        Label!), \(followingNumberLabel.accessibility
        Label!)"

        followingAccessibilityElement.accessibility
        FrameInContainerSpace = followingStackView.
        convert(followingHeadingLabel.frame, to: self).
        union(followingStackView.convert(following
        NumberLabel.frame, to: self))
        elements.append(followingAccessibilityElement)

        postsAccessibilityElement.accessibilityLabel =
        "\(postsHeadingLabel.accessibilityLabel!), \
        (postsNumberLabel.accessibilityLabel!)"

        postsAccessibilityElement.accessibilityFrame
        InContainerSpace = postsStackView.convert
        (postsHeadingLabel.frame, to: self).union(posts
        StackView.convert(postsNumberLabel.frame, to:
        self))
        elements.append(postsAccessibilityElement)

        return elements
    }
}
```

Now when using VoiceOver, the focus will behave in a much more logical way, and you will need less swipes to navigate the app, as you can see in Figure 4-6:

Figure 4-6. *Sequence of the behavior when navigating the UI in Figure 4-4 after grouping some UI elements creating your own array of accessibility elements*

Custom actions

There should always exist an easy way for performing any available action in the app. But sometimes there are features for power users that allow you to perform some of those actions with shortcuts or gestures. An example of this could be the possibility of marking as read, flag, or archive an email by swiping left or right. But it turns out that actually VoiceOver overrides those gestures for navigating to the previous or next accessible element.

Some other times there are lists with rows of information with actions available for each one of those items that you may want to avoid reading every time when using VoiceOver because it could get very repetitive for the user. An example of this scenario would be a Twitter client app, or similar, where you can always reply, retweet, like, share, etc. Reading all those options for every single tweet would be very redundant. You would probably have to swipe right or left many times to get to the next or previous tweet too. Plus, while visually it is clear that those actions belong to a particular tweet, because they are inside one single cell, with VoiceOver it could be unclear if those actions belong to the current tweet or the following one if we break that encapsulation, especially if the user is exploring the screen instead of swiping from one accessibility element to the other.

A possible solution for those two use cases, and others, is the use of custom actions. You can change the buttons so they are no longer accessible to VoiceOver and then you can create an array of accessibility custom actions for all those options, with a name and a selector to perform that action, and either add it to the cell/view or override that property.

```
// Configure custom actions
accessibilityCustomActions = [UIAccessibilityCustomAction
(name: like, target: self, selector: #selector(likeButton
Pressed(_:))),
UIAccessibilityCustomAction(name: share, target: self,
selector: #selector(shareButtonPressed(_:)))]
```

The selector just needs to get the custom action as a parameter and return a boolean as whether that action was or not successful:

```
@objc func likeButtonPressed(_ action: UIAccessibilityCustom
Action) -> Bool {
        var success = false
        // Perform action
        return success
}
```

And new in iOS 13, you can create actions that take an action handler instead of a target and selector. So you could write something like this:

```
var userCustomAction = UIAccessibilityCustomAction
(name: viewModel.userName) { (customAction) -> Bool in
        var success = false
        // Perform action
        return success
}

accessibilityCustomActions?.append(userCustomAction)
```

When doing this, a hint saying "Actions available" gets vocalized by VoiceOver. When swiping up and down, those configured actions get read and can be actioned with a double tap. With the code example, a swipe up would say "Share," another swipe would say "Like," and if double tapping it would execute *likeButtonPressed(_:)*.

And because it is an array of actions, you can always append more of them if the configuration changes:

```
// Append more custom actions
accessibilityCustomActions?.append(UIAccessibilityCustomAction
(name: viewModel.userName, target: self, selector: #selector
(userButtonPressed(_:))))
```

And the best thing, your app will now be much easier to navigate with VoiceOver because with just one swipe the user will be able to get to the next logical piece of content, and it will now be clear what content the user is performing those actions with.

This has also the advantage of making these custom actions easily available for Switch Control users and, new in iOS 13, to Full Keyboard Access and Voice Control users too.

In the case of actions hidden behind custom gestures, like swipes or long taps, the Switch Control menu is probably powerful enough to allow the user to perform such actions. However, using custom actions can first improve discoverability and second make your app more usable (Figure 4-7). It can sometimes reduce the wait time or number of interactions needed by more than 60%, as the custom actions become available in the first page of the Switch Control menu.

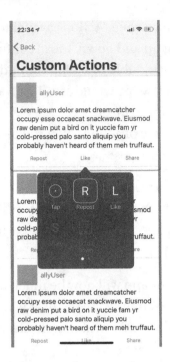

Figure 4-7. *Example of the Switch Control menu when adding custom actions*

Is VoiceOver running?

It is possible to check if some of the assistive technologies are running or even get notifications when the configuration changes. So, for example, you can check if VoiceOver is running or get notified when it gets enabled or disabled. This is useful in the case your UI needs some sort of adaptation for VoiceOver users. Apple suggests in the documentation that you may want to check if VoiceOver is running, for example, if you display UI elements that briefly overlay other parts of your UI and that you could make persistent for VoiceOver users. It is probably a better approach for UI elements not to be ephemeral. This approach can make your UI more usable for any of your users. However, you have the possibility of providing a different experience for VoiceOver users, if you need to.

```
// Check if VoiceOver is running
if UIAccessibility.isVoiceOverRunning {
    // Do something here
}
```

I actually think this can be useful for doing some optimizations. For example, imagine that you have a long list of elements in a table view or collection view and you have to build some accessibility labels, maybe using some number or date formatters, and also create an array of custom actions, etc. It can get a bit expensive, especially if you are building them as the user scrolls.

When doing this, though, you have to consider a couple things. The first one is to listen to the accessibility notifications to see if the user's preferences around accessibility change during the use of the app.

```
// Add observer to get notified when VoiceOver gets enabled
NotificationCenter.default.addObserver(self, selector:
#selector(configureAccessibility), name: UIAccessibility.
voiceOverStatusDidChangeNotification, object: nil)
```

The second one is to think if whatever you are putting inside the "if" statement could be useful for other users. For example, if you are creating custom actions for a cell, these are extremely useful for Switch Control users too, and you could also check if Switch Control is running.

```
// Check if Voice Control is on
if UIAccessibility.isSwitchControlRunning {
    // Do something here
}
```

UISwitch

A very common UI pattern in apps, especially in the settings sections, is to have *UITableViewCell*s with a *UISwitch* (Figure 4-8). When using VoiceOver, the ideal behavior is for the whole cell to be one accessible element. The accessibility label could be the text in the cell. The accessibility value, the value of the *UISwitch*. And you should be able to toggle the switch by double tapping the screen when the cell is focused. You can also hint the user that you can double tap to toggle the value of the cell.

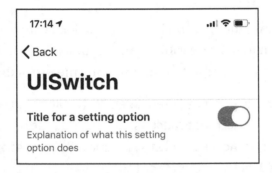

Figure 4-8. *Example of a UI with a UISwitch*

This is exactly the behavior you will find in the General Settings of the system and in any Apple app. It is actually a common mistake not to do so, and you'll find lots of apps that first read the text in the cell, and when swiping right, VoiceOver focuses on the switch and reads the labels again. For a cell that looks like the one in the image, you could create a subclass of *UITableViewCell* that reproduces the expected behavior like this:

```
// Create Settings Cell
class SwitchTableViewCell: UITableViewCell {
    @IBOutlet weak var settingTitleLabel: UILabel!
    @IBOutlet weak var settingSubtitleLabel: UILabel!
    @IBOutlet weak var settingSwitch: UISwitch!
```

```swift
override func awakeFromNib() {
    super.awakeFromNib()
    isAccessibilityElement = true
}

override var accessibilityLabel: String? {
    get { "\(settingTitleLabel.accessibilityLabel ?? ""). \
    (settingSubtitleLabel.accessibilityLabel ?? "")" }
    set {}
}

override var accessibilityTraits: UIAccessibilityTraits {
    get { settingSwitch.accessibilityTraits }
    set {}
}

override var accessibilityValue: String? {
    get { settingSwitch.accessibilityValue }
    set {}
}

override func accessibilityActivate() -> Bool {
    settingSwitch.isOn = !settingSwitch.isOn
    return true
}
}
```

Making the cell itself accessible prevents VoiceOver from focusing the labels and switch separately. Overriding the traits and the value helps VoiceOver vocalize the whole cell as if it was a switch. Overriding the accessibility label lets you concatenate both the title and subtitle accessibility labels. And overriding *accessibilityActivate()* allows you to capture the double tap event and manually toggle the switch value.

Summary

- The Perform Escape action lets users go back with a "scrub" on the screen with two fingers.

- The Magic Tap is a double tap with two fingers that triggers the most important action of the current section of the app.

- You can specify a view as modal in terms of accessibility, so VoiceOver ignores any siblings of that view.

- You can post notifications to let VoiceOver know that the screen or layout changed, or even to make announcements.

- It is possible to group several elements into a new accessibility element.

- Custom actions will make VoiceOver experiences less verbose and more structured, and they will help Switch Control users perform those actions with less effort.

With this information we have all we need to create amazing experiences for our VoiceOver users. In the next chapter, we will start exploring how to create apps that let the users configure large font sizes and how to tweak the layout to adapt accordingly.

CHAPTER 5

Dynamic Type

Dynamic Type is probably one of the accessibility features that most of us, as iOS users, will use at some point in our lives. It allows the user to change the preferred font size in the system settings. Learn how to create a UI that can adapt properly to very large text sizes, if the user decides to use them.

What is Dynamic Type?

Dynamic Type is another important accessibility feature. It is a mechanism that lets your UI adapt to different font sizes depending on the user's preferences. Supported font sizes go from *.extraSmall* to *.extraExtraExtraLarge*. And you can enable 5 extra accessibility sizes: from *.accessibilityMedium* to *.accessibilityExtraExtraExtraLarge*. Imagine that you download an app and the font is so minuscule that it makes everything very difficult to read. This is exactly how elder people feel when using almost any app, for example. And it is something that is going to happen to most of us. That is why it is so important to implement Dynamic Type properly, so people can change their settings to accommodate the font size to their needs.

iOS 11 introduced some great accessibility improvements. As an example, the operating system's UI and the iOS stock apps started extensively using bigger and bolder fonts, which are easier to read.

© Daniel Devesa Derksen-Staats 2019
D. D. Derksen-Staats, *Developing Accessible iOS Apps*,
https://doi.org/10.1007/978-1-4842-5308-3_5

But more importantly, the support of Dynamic Type throughout the system was hugely improved. Before iOS 11 all the text styles adapted to bigger font sizes. However, only the body text style adapted to the 5 accessibility text sizes. This is not the case since iOS 11 anymore, and now all text styles scale appropriately for all text styles, including the accessibility ones. You can see in the screenshots a comparison between iOS 10 and iOS 11. There is a big difference in how this example app is rendered when using larger accessibility sizes. How much better does the app look when all the different text styles grow at the same time? So, don't be surprised if your app does look different in different iOS versions for users that have this feature enabled, as Apple may keep improving its support in the future.

As you can see in Figure 5-1, iOS 11 simplified the adoption of larger accessibility sizes. Notice how even the Settings screen for selecting your preferred accessibility text size itself is much better adapted in iOS 11 than it was in iOS 10 (Figure 5-2). Also notice that the label next to the switch is bigger too and the layout slightly changes, so the switch is placed below the label so that there is a little more room for the text. We'll have a look at how you can achieve this in your app later in this chapter.

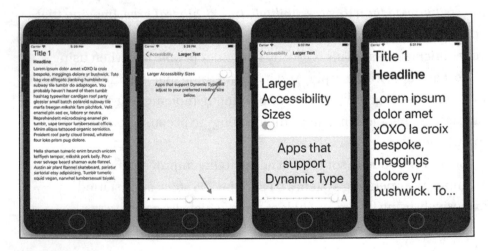

Figure 5-1. *Example of accessibility text sizes support in iOS 11*

Figure 5-2. *Example of accessibility text sizes support in iOS 10*

If you are using native iOS components in a standard way and any of the built-in text styles (Headline, Title 1, Title 2, Title 3, Body, Footnote, etc.) for the text in your app, you will get lots of these improvements either "for free" or with very little effort. And of course, Auto Layout is your friend here to make your UI properly resize itself and adapt to accommodate text with a much larger font scale.

Supporting larger text

The first step for supporting Dynamic Type is to configure your labels to use the preferred font for a supported text style. There are 11 different text styles, from "Large Title" to "Footnote," with others like "Headline" or "Body" in between, and the code to do this looks like this:

```
// Use of preferred font for a text style
postLabel.font = UIFont.preferredFont(forTextStyle: .body)
```

If you also check the box in Interface Builder for "Automatically Adjust Font" (Figure 5-3), you will also pick up changes if the user modifies their accessibility preferences in iOS Settings. You needed to be listening to a notification in previous iOS versions to achieve that.

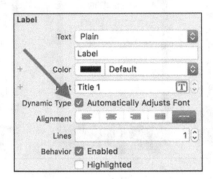

Figure 5-3. *Automatically Adjust Font option in the Interface Builder menu in Xcode*

If you aren't using Interface Builder and prefer to keep things in code, in the example of a *UILabel*, you can write:

```
// Automatically adjust size if user preference changes
postLabel.adjustsFontForContentSizeCategory = true
```

Oddly enough, Apple didn't enforce this as the default option, so you have to remember to do any of those two steps for your labels to automatically adjust them when the user changes the font size preferences while using your app.

It is also important to let the labels have multiple lines. If possible, just set the number of lines to 0. I know, it is a bit strange, but 0 basically means no limit. The label will have as many lines as it needs. If you need to set a limit, please check how it looks with the larger font size. To change the number of lines, you can do it in both Interface Builder and code:

```
// No limit in number of lines
postLabel.numberOfLines = 0
```

If you have any design constraints, you can also have a different number of lines for the default text sizes and for the larger accessibility text sizes. We will see how to do that later in the chapter.

Custom fonts

And if your app uses custom fonts? It used to be more complicated, but, again with iOS 11 accessibility improvements, you can now use the *UIFontMetrics* class to scale your font based on the user's text size preference. Implementing this for a *UILabel* is as simple as this:

```
// Map custom font to system's text styles
postLabel.font = UIFontMetrics(forTextStyle: .title1).
scaledFont(for: customFont)
```

You can also map how your font scales to the default text styles by doing something like:

```
// Scale a custom font with user's selected preferences
postLabel.font = UIFontMetrics.default.scaledFont(for: customFont)
```

Adjusting your user interface to better adapt to big font sizes

I can't stress enough the importance of testing your app for the worst-case scenario. It is really easy to oversee cases that in principle it looks as if it should just work but surprisingly it doesn't. How many screens of your app are composed of a very simple view containing just some text and maybe an icon and/or a button? I'm thinking especially about loading, offline, and error screens, present in almost every app. But you could have other more complicated screens that still you may think they will fit in the size of the screen, like simple profile pages, custom alerts, popovers, etc.

In this case it is worth checking how they would look when using the biggest accessibility text size (and fix the UI in case the content doesn't fit in the screen when using this configuration).

It is also a good idea to check how it would look with a larger text, so you are safe in case you change the text in the future or if you localize the app in different languages. For example, it is very likely that languages like Spanish or German may require more room to be entirely displayed. Let's have a look at how to make your app flexible and test with longer text now.

For something as simple as the layout in the screenshot in Figure 5-4, if the user decides to use the largest text size, the layout would not fit in the screen, it would break and the "Retry" button could not be tapped as it would not be visible.

Figure 5-4. *Comparison of an app with the default text size and the largest text size*

The easiest solution for this is to probably put those views inside a scroll view. If you are using Interface Builder, that is pretty straightforward to do. Select all the UI components, go to "Editor," in Xcode's top menu, then "Embed in...," and embed everything into a view first and then repeat the process to embed the new view into a scroll view (Figure 5-5).

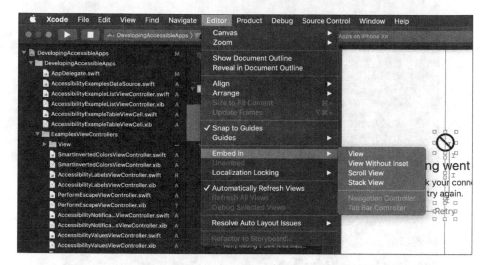

Figure 5-5. *Menu that lets you embed the selected views in a scroll view*

You'll still need to add some more constraints from the inner components to the outer ones, but the relations in between the initial components will persist. Your Interface Builder *xib* or *storyboard* file will look something similar to Figure 5-6.

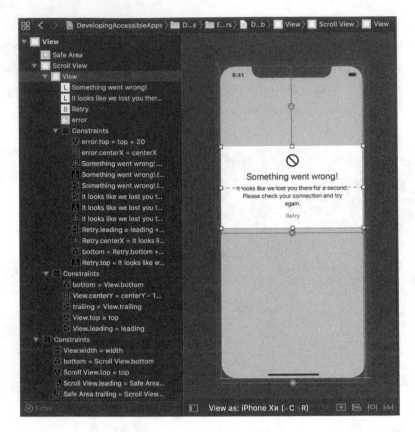

Figure 5-6. *Adding missing constraints in Interface Builder*

Now the content looks as you wanted for smaller text sizes, but it will allow the user to scroll to see all the information if they need a much bigger text font. If you find it tricky to deal with constraints, another simple way of achieving a similar result is to use a vertical stack view inside a scroll view or, since iOS 13, you can also use *SwiftUI* for a more declarative approach in code.

For trying out how your UI would behave with a longer text, this is a very useful trick. Just click your app's icon and name on the top left corner in Xcode, select "Edit Scheme..." and go to "Run" and then "Options." You can select the language of the system when debugging an app in the simulator (Figure 5-7). If you scroll to the bottom, you will find a pseudolanguage called "Double-Length" that will do just that, double all the strings in your app.

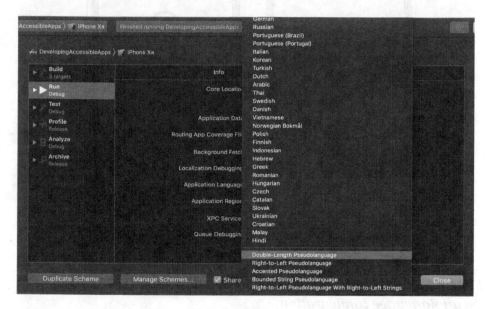

Figure 5-7. *How to set your simulator to use Double-Length Pseudolanguage*

If you run the app in the simulator with the previous configuration, the app will look like Figure 5-8.

You will notice that there are some other options like "Right-to-Left Pseudolanguage" that will come really handy if you want to see how your app would render for right-to-left languages like Arabic but keeping the text in your default language. "Bounded String Pseudolanguage" will show you which strings come from a *NSLocalizedString* and which don't, so it is easy to find strings that are not localized.

Figure 5-8. *Example app running with Double-Length Pseudolanguage configuration*

You may also be wondering how it is that the image was resized together with the text. It is a good idea to scale glyphs that appear next to text, so the users can see them too and the UI still looks balanced. It is very easy to do, and we will talk about it in the next chapter.

Different layouts for different font sizes

There are times when your default layout is just not going to work with bigger font sizes. I have found this a lot, especially when using table views or collection views, in which it is quite common to have an image followed by some text, maybe the title, a small summary, and more information about that particular item (Figure 5-9). You may also remember Apple's example in Settings, where they move the *UISwitch* under the title instead of keeping it on its right so there is more room for the text.

Figure 5-9. *Example app that doesn't adapt well to big font sizes*

In cases like this, if you make the font very big, there is very little space for the text to be displayed, and the app becomes almost useless for the user. It is not a great experience to show less information just because the user needs a bigger font. You should aim to avoid any unnecessary truncation or overlap of the text with other elements of the UI, and your app should look beautiful at all text sizes. One solution to this issue could be to use an alternative layout.

The first step is to use self-sizing cells. You want the height of the different cells to resize automatically depending on the size of its content. A similar approach is also valid for collection views. For using self-sizing views, you just need to follow a few steps. First, you have to use Auto

Layout when defining the layout of your cells. Second, you also have to set the estimated row height for the average cell to your best guess. Finally, set the actual row height to automatic. This also applies to section headers and footers.

```
// Configuring table view to use self-sizing cells
tableView.estimatedRowHeight = 100.0
tableView.rowHeight = UITableView.automaticDimension
```

Then, when returning a cell for the table view in the *UITableView* delegate's method, we could check the preferred content size category in the view controller's trait collection. The content size category has a handy property to check if the user is using an accessibility category, and, if this was the case, we could return an alternative cell with a more appropriate layout. The code would look something like this:

```
// Offer alternative layout if the user needs accessibility
font sizes
extension DynamicTypeAdaptiveViewController:
UITableViewDelegate {
        func tableView(_ tableView: UITableView, cellForRowAt
        indexPath: IndexPath) -> UITableViewCell {
                let cell: UITableViewCell

                if traitCollection.preferredContentSize
                Category.isAccessibilityCategory {
                        cell = tableView.dequeueReusableCell
                        (withIdentifier: AlternativeImageTable
                        ViewCell.identifier, for: indexPath)
                } else {
                        cell = tableView.dequeueReusableCell
                        (withIdentifier: ImageTableViewCell.
                        identifier, for: indexPath)
                }
```

```
        return cell
    }
}
```

UIContentSizeCategory, apart from letting you know if the user has selected an accessibility category, defines all the available sizes from *.extraSmall* to *.accessibilityExtraExtraExtraLarge* and lets you compare them by conforming to the *Equatable* protocol. This is very useful in case you want to change your layout starting from a certain size, like *.large*, even if it is still not considered an accessibility size. Your condition in that case would look something like this:

```
// Scale a custom font with user's selected preferences
if traitCollection.preferredContentSizeCategory >= .large {}
```

Now, when the user changes the font size preference, the UI will adapt in a way that you can still access all the information (Figure 5-10):

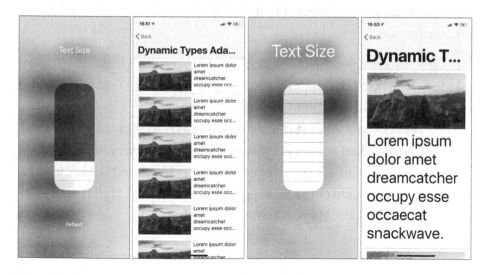

Figure 5-10. *Example app that works well with big font sizes*

You could also use this technique to do other minor modifications, for example, having a different available number of lines for the different labels in the UI, letting the user have a bit more space for text if the text size is bigger. Or you could even have two separate sets of Auto Layout constraints, if you prefer to write your layout in code. When doing so, you can just activate/deactivate the appropriate one. One way of doing it would be to have, for example, three arrays: one for defining common constraints, another one for the default constraints, and a last one for the alternative constraints:

```
// Define array with constraints
private var commonConstraints: [NSLayoutConstraint] = []
private var defaultConstraints: [NSLayoutConstraint] = []
private var alternativeConstraints: [NSLayoutConstraint] = []
```

Once you have defined all the constraints, you can override the method that tells you when a trait collection has changed. If the current accessibility category is different than the previous one, you can update your constraints:

```
// Listen to changes in the trait collection
override func traitCollectionDidChange(_ previousTrait
Collection: UITraitCollection?) {
        let isAccessibilityCategory = traitCollection.preferred
        ContentSizeCategory.isAccessibilityCategory
        if isAccessibilityCategory != previousTraitCollection?.
        preferredContentSizeCategory.isAccessibilityCategory {
                updateLayoutConstraints()
        }
}
```

And finally, as we anticipated, you need to activate or deactivate the desired constraints stored in the previously defined arrays:

```
// Activate/deactivate the appropriate constraints
private func updateLayoutConstraints() {
        NSLayoutConstraint.activate(commonConstraints)
        if traitCollection.preferredContentSizeCategory.
        isAccessibilityCategory {
                NSLayoutConstraint.deactivate(defaultConstraints)
                NSLayoutConstraint.activate(alternative
                Constraints)
        } else {
                NSLayoutConstraint.deactivate(alternative
                Constraints)
                NSLayoutConstraint.activate(defaultConstraints)
        }
}
```

Why should you support even the largest accessibility text size?

It is very important to support the full range of dynamic type text sizes, including all the accessibility text sizes. Some people may think the screenshot on the right is ridiculously big, but it is actually what some of your users may need. If you have low vision, a bigger enough font might help you use your device without needing a screen reader at all, or at least that often. Figure 5-11 tries to exemplify that scenario, simulating how some users with low vision could probably still read and use your app with the biggest possible font, while smaller ones would be totally unreadable. And as you have seen, most of times it takes very little effort to support.

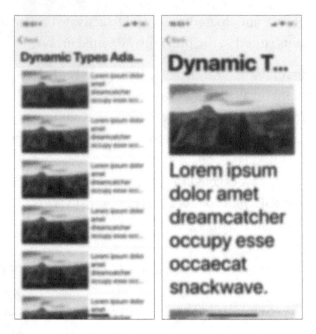

Figure 5-11. *Proving the importance of large text sizes for low-vision users*

Dynamic Type support in your web content

Sometimes it is just convenient to use static HTML content in a web view to show some information to your users. You can find this mostly for terms and conditions, FAQs, privacy policies, etc. Luckily, there is a way for the text of your web content to adapt to the user's text size preferences. There are Apple-specific CSS values for defining font families. These will just work on Apple devices, so it is very important to specify fallback fonts if you are planning to use this content in other platforms. For example, if you want to use the body style for the *body* in your HTML and also the headline style for *h1* or the *footnote* style, you could define something like this in your CSS stylesheet:

```css
body {
    font: -apple-system-body;
}
h1 {
    font: -apple-system-headline;
    color: darkblue;
}
.footnote {
    font: -apple-system-footnote;
    color: gray;
}
```

And your HTML could look something like this:

```html
<!DOCTYPE html>
<html>
<head>
<meta name="viewport" content="width=device-width,initial-
scale=1">
<link rel="stylesheet" href="styles.css"/>
</head>
<body>
<h1>This is an H1 header</h1>
<p>Lorem ipsum dolor amet twee distillery narwhal id pork
belly chartreuse fixie aliqua hella vexillologist schlitz
letterpress.</p>
<p>Fam non iPhone keytar plaid pabst 8-bit edison bulb cornhole
et ad tattooed tilde ex.</p>
<div class="footnote">This is a footer text</div>
</body>
</html>
```

Unfortunately, the web content won't get resized if the content size changes, so your best option may be to listen to these changes and reload the web page if necessary. You can find more information about the different system font styles supported in the WebKit web page: https://webkit.org/blog/3709/using-the-system-font-in-web-content/.

If you save the previous CSS code in a file called "styles.css" and your HTML code in one called "dynamic-type-example.html" and you add those files to your Xcode's project, this is the code that loads the html file in a web view and reloads it if the content size category changes:

```
// Reload web view if content size category changes
class WebViewController: UIViewController {
    @IBOutlet weak var webView: WKWebView!

    override func viewDidLoad() {
        super.viewDidLoad()
        if let baseURL = Bundle.main.resourceURL {
            let fileURL = baseURL.appendingPathComponent
            ("dynamic-type-example.html")
            webView?.loadFileURL(fileURL, allowingReadAccessTo:
            fileURL)
        }

        NotificationCenter.default.addObserver(self, selector:
        #selector(contentSizeCategoryDidChange(_:)), name:
        UIContentSizeCategory.didChangeNotification, object:
        nil)
    }

    @objc private func contentSizeCategoryDidChange
    (_ notification: Notification) {
        webView?.reload()
    }
}
```

Summary

- Dynamic Type is a feature that, when implemented, lets your users configure their preferred font size from the system Settings.

- There are 7 font sizes (from *.extraSmall* to *.extraExtraExtraLarge*), plus 5 accessibility font sizes (*.accessibilityMedium* to *.accessibilityExtraExtraExtraLarge*) that can be enabled from the Accessibility settings page.

- For supporting Dynamic Type, you can use the preferred font for one of the defined styles (Headline, Title 1, Title 2, Title 3, Body, Footnote, etc.).

- It is possible to use custom fonts with Dynamic Type by getting a scaled font using the *UIFontMetrics* class.

- You can use different layouts for different content size categories.

- Web content can also be scaled for different content size categories.

VoiceOver and Dynamic Type are probably two of the biggest topics to consider when building accessible apps. But they are not the only ones. In the next chapter, we will learn how to support many other accessibility options available in the Accessibility settings.

CHAPTER 6

Other accessibility features and good practices

We have covered so far how to make your apps play nicely when users turn on VoiceOver or when they decide to use a different font size to the default one. But there are many other accessibility settings that the user can configure that we will need to properly support. And there are also other best practices that might not be directly related to any iOS accessibility feature but that are worth taking into account too. This chapter will cover many other important features that are sometimes overseen by developers but that can bring the accessibility support of your app to the next level.

Invert Colors

A less obvious accessibility feature is the possibility of inverting the colors of the screen. Most apps opt for dark text colors over a light background. That can make the screen very bright and cause discomfort to some people that would find it much easier to read light text over dark backgrounds.

Inverting the colors of the screen does the trick in this case. This option has always been available in the Accessibility settings in iOS, but the experience wasn't great because it inverted the whole UI, even images or videos that would look as if they were in negative and become quite hard to see properly.

In iOS 11, Apple also introduced Smart Invert Colors. It is actually really easy to implement in your app. There is a new accessibility property that lets any UI component opt out from being inverted when the user has this setting enabled.

For opting out an image view from having its colors inverted, it would be as easy as doing this:

```
// Avoid image from having its colors inverted
imageView.accessibilityIgnoresInvertColors = true
```

For some reason Apple has decided to keep the Classic Invert Colors feature. Maybe just in case some apps misuse or don't implement this feature correctly? In Figure 6-1 you can see the difference between the old Classic Invert Colors mode and the new Smart Invert Colors option. As you can see, Apple itself excludes some of the native components from being inverted so they are more visible. You can see an example in Figure 6-1, where the *UISwitch* is much more visible when using Smart Invert Colors, especially when toggled off.

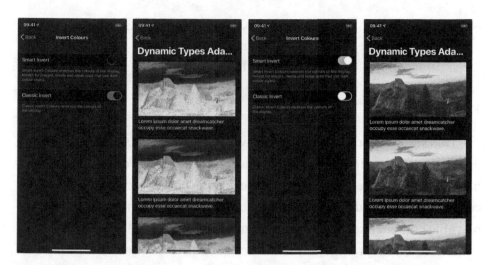

Figure 6-1. *Comparison between Classic Invert Colors and Smart Invert Colors*

Another thing to really keep in mind is that, if your app's default choice is the opposite, that is, white or light color text over black or dark backgrounds, the Invert Colors mode will still invert your apps colors. This would achieve the exact opposite of what the user is trying to do. And to avoid them constantly switching on or off Invert Colors depending on the color palette of each app, you have two options. One is to opt out most of the UI components of your app from being inverted. The other one is to both detect if the user has chosen to invert colors – and to listen to a notification in case that changes – and correct the colors yourself. Notice how Apple's dark apps like the calculator, stocks, or compass apps are still dark when enabling Invert Colors.

```
// React to Invert Colors preferences
NotificationCenter.default.addObserver(self, selector:
#selector(accessibilityInvertedColorsChanged), name:
Notification.Name.UIAccessibilityInvertColorsStatusDidChange,
object: nil)
```

```
@objc func accessibilityInvertedColorsChanged() {
        if UIAccessibilityIsInvertColorsEnabled() {
                    // Manually invert colors of your view
        }
}
```

This snippet of code is also handy when you have a mix of dark/ light text colors on top of light/dark background colors. For example, you may have a table view in which each cell represents some media from a collection. We could have white cells for photos and text and black cells for playable content like audio or video. In that case, you can choose the color of the cells that represent playable content to be the same as the other ones when Invert Colors is enabled. That way, when colors are inverted, all the cells will behave the same way.

Signaling events or contextual information

It is a great moment to mention a very important accessibility rule, which is try not to signal things in just one way. For example, if the black cells represent playable content but suddenly all the cells look the same when inverting colors, users of this feature won't be able to see that information. On the other hand, if those cells also have a play icon and a duration, it will still be obvious that those cells represent a different kind of media. The same would happen with VoiceOver: if the only difference between cells representing different types of content is the color, and we don't give VoiceOver more information to vocalize that difference, the user will lose some context.

Another example that is quite frequent is signaling something like an error with just a sound or just a color. If I signal something like an error with just a color and no other information, if the user is perhaps color-blind, then that information is going to be lost. If we just used haptic feedback, switch control users would not notice what just happened.

If we just used a sound, deaf users wouldn't be aware of what just happened either. So, for making sure you reach all your users, it is a good idea to communicate dynamic information in more than one way by combining color, icons, text, animations, sound, haptic feedback, etc.

Large Preview

You may have noticed that not all the UI elements in iOS use a larger font when an accessibility font size is set. Such elements include the iOS Navigation Bar and Tab Bar – text sizes remain the same regardless of these settings. This seems to be a conscious design decision from Apple to avoid taking up too much screen space, as that would leave very little real estate for the actual content. But since iOS 11, if you long-press Tab Bar icons, a larger version of the icon and tab name will show in the middle of the screen. The feature isn't widely mentioned in WWDC videos, but it also works with elements of a *UINavigationBar* (like the navigation bar title, back button, or any other bar button item) and *UIToolBar* as well.

This should just work if you are using native navigation components like *UINavigationBar* or *UITabBar*. But for it to show the icons in a nice resolution, you would just need to add your Tab Bar assets in PDF format. Yes, it's not a typo – Apple decided to use PDFs for vector-based images. When adding the PDF to your Asset Catalog in Xcode, simply tick the box for preserving the vector data of the asset in Interface Builder (Figure 6-2). If you don't do that, Xcode will just rasterize the image to any sizes (@1x, @2x, and @3x) that the app might need.

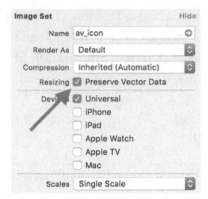

Figure 6-2. *How to preserve vector data on PDF assets*

If, for any reason, your designer cannot provide you with a PDF asset, you can still get the same effect with a larger PNG asset along with the following property on the *UITabBarItem*:

```
// Larger version for the tab bar item image
tabBarItem.largeContentSizeImage = largerImage
```

I haven't found a specific size for this image in Apple's documentation, but 75x75 pixels for an @1x size seems to give a reasonable result.

Figure 6-3 shows how this feature works in Apple Music's app. Up till recently it would just work by default with *UIKit* bars, and you had to implement a similar approach yourself if you wanted to offer a similar experience. But since iOS 13, there are new APIs for adopting the Large Content Viewer with custom elements. I've worked in a few apps that for some reason would implement custom navigation bars and tab bars. Once you go down the route of using custom components, it might not be easy to replace them with *UIKit* ones, but at least now it doesn't necessarily need to come at the cost of a worse accessibility experience for users with low vision.

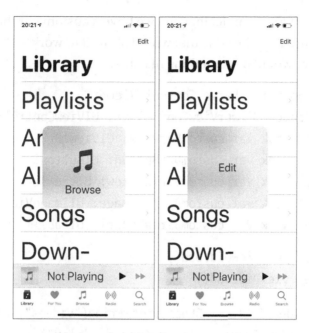

Figure 6-3. *Large Preview example in Apple Music*

But first remember, if your UI can scale using Dynamic Type, you should do it this way whenever possible. Large Content Preview should only be used for situations in which your content would not be able to scale. And the perfect example is, as mentioned, navigation elements or sticky bars and tool bars that could be getting too much real estate from your screen and leaving very little space available for the actual content.

There is a new protocol called *UILargeContentViewerItem* that *UIView*s implement by default. You can mark any views to be shown with the Large Content Viewer by setting the *showsLargeContentViewer* property to *true*, and you can specify the image and text by setting or overriding *largeContentTitle* and/or *largeContentImage* with the desired value. The last thing to do would be to register a *UILargeContentViewerInteraction* interaction to the containing bar with *addInteraction()*, just the same way you would do when adding drag and drop support. It may be easier to

understand with an example. Imagine we have a custom bar that looks like
the one in Figure 6-4. The code that would allow it to work with the Large
Content Viewer would be something like this:

```
// Adopt Support for Large Content Viewer
class LargeContentViewerViewController: UIViewController {
    @IBOutlet weak var customBarView: UIView!
    @IBOutlet weak var customBarButton: UIButton!
    @IBOutlet weak var customBarTabView: UIView!
    @IBOutlet weak var customBarTabImage: UIImageView!
    @IBOutlet weak var customBarTabLabel: UILabel!

    override func viewDidLoad() {
        super.viewDidLoad()

        let videosTitle = NSLocalizedString("Videos", comment: "")
        let videosImage = UIImage(named: "play")

        customBarTabImage.image = videosImage
        customBarTabLabel.text = videosTitle

        if #available(iOS 13.0, *) {
            let largeContentViewerInteraction = UILargeContent
            ViewerInteraction()

            customBarView.addInteraction(largeContentViewer
            Interaction)

            customBarButton.showsLargeContentViewer = true
```

```
        customBarTabView.showsLargeContentViewer = true
        customBarTabView.largeContentImage = videosImage
        customBarTabView.largeContentTitle = videosTitle
    }
  }
}
```

Figure 6-4. *Example of Large Preview implementation*

Notice how certain UI classes like *UIButton* or *UILabel* have default values for the title and image, and you don't have to do anything. However, with a custom *UIView*, you have to specify those yourself.

Scale icons

Ideally, as you've seen in previous examples, you want to scale glyphs that appear next to text. This has two main purposes: it will make the icon also visible for users using bigger font sizes, and it will also keep your UI balanced and looking as good as it does with the default text size.

It can be done in a couple ways for your own custom images and icons. The first one is using Interface Builder, by ticking the box in the Accessibility section for adjusting the image size in an image view (Figure 6-5).

Figure 6-5. *Automatically adjust the image size with large content size categories*

But you can also do it in code. You just need to set the *UIImage* property for adjusting the image size for accessibility content size categories to *true*.

```
// Adjust images for bigger font sizes
iconImage.adjustsImageSizeForAccessibilityContentSizeCategory =
true
```

For both of these cases, it is also important to remember that, as we did for the Large Content Viewer, the best way to avoid the image to blur when resized is to use the PDF format and to check the box to preserve the vector data.

And there is a third way if you are happy to use one of the new SF Symbols introduced in iOS 13. There are thousands of them. They have the benefit of behaving like fonts. Each symbol can be scaled to different sizes but also supports different weights, to match the accompanying text. You can also configure it with a Dynamic Type text style, and it will automatically scale with your text when the user changes the text size preference. You can get an SF Symbol image just by its system name and then specify the preferred symbol configuration to a particular text style that matches your text.

```
// Get SF Symbol Image
iconImageView.image = UIImage(systemName: "xmark.octagon")
iconImageView.preferredSymbolConfiguration = UIImage.Symbol
Configuration(textStyle: .body)
```

If a symbol is not available in the predefined set, your designer can create a custom symbol too. You can find how to do that in the "Introducing SF Symbols" video from the WWDC 2019. If you do that, you will need to access the image with the classic *imageNamed* initializer instead of the new *systemName* one.

Accessibility configurations

As with Smart Invert Colors or when using Dynamic Type, it is basically just a matter of respecting user's preferences in your app and behaving as a good citizen in the iOS ecosystem. If you try some of the accessibility configurations from Settings, you will see that most of them automatically work throughout the system including your app. Some of these examples are **Button Shapes**, which make more clear what UI elements are buttons, usually by underlying them but also highlighting the tab bar button that is selected, and **Increased Contrast**, which increases the color contrast for improving readability. Still, you can detect when the user enables these, in case you want to have better control over these configurations or if you think you can do even better.

However, there are a couple more configurations that will need your help to work properly.

Reduce Motion

Some people may feel a bit sick or just find it difficult to concentrate when too many things are moving around the screen. They may opt then to Reduce Motion in Settings. You'll immediately notice that some of the system's animations are much more subtle.

```
// Check if the user wants reduced motion
if UIAccessibility.isReduceMotionEnabled {}
```

You can also check if the user changed this preference by listening to the corresponding notification:

```
// Get notification if the user changes motion preference
NotificationCenter.default.addObserver(self, selector:
#selector(handleReduceMotion(_:)), name: UIAccessibility.
reduceMotionStatusDidChangeNotification, object: nil)

@objc func handleReduceMotion(_ sender: Any) {
        // Enable/Disable motion in your app
}
```

In my previous teams, I very often had the discussion on whether we should auto-play or preview the videos in the app. In my opinion it is most of times not a good idea, and from the accessibility point of view, you should always try to avoid it for many reasons. But iOS 13 made this issue a bit easier to deal with and introduced a great new Accessibility setting: Auto-Play Video Previews. The API is also public, so you can adopt it in your app too.

```
// Check if the user has autoplay enabled
if UIAccessibility.isVideoAutoplayEnabled {}
```

It is possible that you already had an in-app setting for this option. In that case, you can decide whether to keep it or not, but it would probably be a good idea to mirror the user's global preference as the default value, so that the app behaves as the user chose in the general settings. I would probably even disable the local preference if the user decided to disable this option in the general settings too. If then that in-app preference gets enabled later though, you could override that option in your app, because the user voluntarily chose to do so. To help you with this, and as you can do with the Reduce Motion preference, you can also observe this preference for getting notifications in the case the user decides to change it:

```
// Get notification if the user changes autoplay preference
NotificationCenter.default.addObserver(self, selector: #sele
ctor(handleAutoplayStatusChange(_:)), name: UIAccessibility.
videoAutoplayStatusDidChangeNotification, object: nil)

@objc func handleAutoplayStatusChange(_
notification:Notification) {
        // Enable/Disable video autoplay
}
```

Another motion-related setting introduced in iOS 13 is cross-fade transitions when navigating through the apps and the system, instead of the classic lateral slides. As long as you are using *UIKit* standard navigation, this will automatically work for you.

Reduce Transparency

Transparency and blurring have been a big part of the visual design identity of iOS since iOS 7, and it helps establish hierarchy and order. In words of Jony Ive: "translucency gives you a sense of your context." But for some people, particularly with low vision, it can have a negative impact in legibility. That is why Apple provides us with an accessibility setting to reduce transparency when possible. A great example of the application of this feature is Spotlight, because not only do they eliminate the transparency but they also get the main color of the background, so that it can still feel personalized and contextual but reducing the noise and improving contrast.

Some native components like navigation bars or tab bars will honor this configuration. If you use *UIBlurEffect*'s *UIVisualEffect*, the Reduce Transparency configuration will also be respected. But if you are applying some alpha to a view's background, it won't. In that case, you can first check if the user has enabled Reduce Transparency for applying the normal alpha or for making it less transparent or just opaque.

```
// Check if the user wants reduced transparency
if UIAccessibility.isReduceTransparencyEnabled {}
```

And, the same way you can do with most accessibility settings, as seen with Reduce Motion or Reduce Transparency too, you can add observers to get notified when the Reduce Transparency preference changes.

```
// Get notification if the user changes Reduce Transparency
preference
NotificationCenter.default.addObserver(self, selector:
#selector(handleReduceTransparency), name: UIAccessibility.
reduceTransparencyStatusDidChangeNotification, object: nil)

@objc func handleReduceTransparency(_ sender: Any) {
        // Reduce transparency in your app if necessary
}
```

Differentiate without color

We've seen how important it is to signal relevant information in more than one way, and not just rely on things like color because, among other things, color-blind users could not be able to properly interpret what you are trying to say. But if there is any feature in your app where you really need to differentiate things by color for most users, that could happen in some games, for example, there is a new API in iOS 13 to know if the user is explicitly asking for a differentiation without color:

```
// Check if the user needs differentiation without color
if UIAccessibility.shouldDifferentiateWithoutColor {}
```

Imagine a game like Uno, where cards have numbers and colors, and the next user has to throw a card with the same number or color that there is in the table. You could check for this preference and add color alphabet symbols like they do with their ColorADD version of the game that is color-blind accessible.

Closed captioning enabled

If your app has video playback capabilities, this can be an interesting one for you, especially if your videos support subtitles and closed captioning. There is also a *UIAccessibility* property to let you know if the user prefers this feature enabled by default. So, if it is *true*, you could toggle on the closed captions in your video player component:

```
if UIAccessibility.isClosedCaptioningEnabled {
        //Enable subtitles in video player
}
```

If your video also supports subtitles for the deaf and hard of hearing, that is great! You should enable those if possible.

Some other good practices

Making your app accessible doesn't only mean using the accessibility tools and APIs available in the system. It is also important to understand your users and follow a set of guidelines and good practices.

Accessibility guidelines

WCAG 2.0: It stands for Web Content Accessibility Guidelines. Despite being, as the name indicates, Web focused, the general principles also apply to app. It is developed by the World Wide Web Consortium (W3C), and it is the gold standard of accessibility. You can find all the necessary information here: `www.w3.org/WAI/standards-guidelines/wcag/`.

BBC Mobile Accessibility Guidelines: It is a set of guidelines created by the BBC, it is technology agnostic, and it includes anything related to the development of mobile webs and hybrid and native apps. It can be a bit less intimidating than jumping straight into the WCAG guidelines. And the great thing is that you'll find code examples and testing procedures, also for iOS: `www.bbc.co.uk/accessibility/forproducts/`.

There is a tool in Xcode that will help you find if your app is not following some of these basic principles. It is called Accessibility Inspector, and we will talk more about it in Chapter 7 about testing. But for now, let's see what we can do to avoid common mistakes and make our app follow some of these guidelines to create more accessible apps that will pass any Accessibility Inspector audit.

Contrast ratio

The contrast between content (text or icons) and its background is very important when it comes to perceivability. As colors get closer to each other, they become much more difficult to distinguish, and, in the case of text, it worsens its readability. The highest contrast ratio you can get is with black over white, which is a 21:1, and it works perfectly at all text sizes. The minimum contrast you should use is 4.5:1 for normal text and 3:1 for larger text and graphics. It is important to know that the same contrast ratio doesn't work for all the text sizes. As text gets smaller, letters bleed together more easily, and a higher contrast is required to keep readability.

There is a built-in tool in Accessibility Inspector that follows the WCAG, and there are also many online calculators that will help you find the right color for keeping an appropriate contrast ratio, depending on the color of the background and the text size and weight.

Hit areas

For any tappable area like buttons, they should be at least 44pt x 44pt – that is, about a 9-square-millimeter area – and at least 32 points apart from each other. Keeping them a bit separate from each other will reduce the chances of users hitting the incorrect button. People with tremors or shaking of the hands, and also users with low vision, are more likely to make mistakes in small or overlapping buttons. Don't make people tap tiny things, it is just frustrating!

Images with text

It is a bad idea for multiple reasons and yet you see it in many apps. The text will not be read by VoiceOver, for example, and it is not localizable. Of course, there are workarounds and you can provide an accessibility label with a localized text and even replace the image depending on the language of the user. VoiceOver can now even recognize some text in images and read back the possible text to the user. However, it is not very scalable. You'll need to create an image for each language every time you want to do a single change, or it will make releasing new languages harder because you'll need one more asset to prepare. It is easy to miss, and it makes it more difficult to spot contrast ratio issues, for example. And more importantly, the text won't scale with Dynamic Type. It is often done with fancy headers and buttons or even in kid's games. *UILabel* and *UIButton* are highly customizable and will help you have a more maintainable and accessible app.

Summary

- When the user enables Smart Invert Colors, you can exclude images and videos from being inverted for a better user experience.

- Preserve vector data from PDF icons for better supporting Large Content Viewer.

- Since iOS 13, you can support Large Content Viewer with custom navigation bars, tab bars, and tool bars.

- You can scale icons with your text when using large content size categories.

- Take into account if the user enables Reduce Motion, Reduce Transparency, Differentiate with Color, or Closed Captioning.

- Follow accessibility guidelines like WCAG and the BBC Mobile Accessibility Guidelines.

- Make sure that the contrast ratio in the different sections of your app is good enough, that there are no small-hit areas or overlapping buttons, and that you don't use images with text.

Up till now we have learned different ways of improving the accessibility of your app. But how can we find what can be improved or how can we check that our changes worked as expected? It all starts and ends with testing. And that is what the next chapter is about.

CHAPTER 7

Testing

Auditing your app is the most important step to make sure you've achieved a great experience when using the app with assistive technologies. We'll go through some of the tools and processes to properly test an app for accessibility, such as the Accessibility Inspector, Screen Curtain, the Rotor, etc.

Controlling VoiceOver

If you are testing the navigation of your app with VoiceOver, but you are not interested in what VoiceOver says for the moment – maybe you are just looking at how the focus behaves when navigating your app – or you are surrounded by more people in the office and don't have your headphones with you, you can use VoiceOver without voice. A double tap with three fingers will mute/bring back VoiceOver's voice.

On the other hand, if you are demoing something but you need to speak or someone comes to speak to you while using VoiceOver, you can pause/resume VoiceOver with a single tap with two fingers.

Screen curtain

In Chapter 1 we asked you: could you use your app with your eyes closed? It is now time to prove it. There is a way of using VoiceOver with the screen of your device off. It is enabled/disabled by a triple tap with three fingers.

It is the fairest way of testing VoiceOver and it will help you empathize more with your users. If you can make it through the main flows of your app easily, that would be an excellent sign. On the other hand, it will give you, as we mentioned, another perspective of your app. If you find it difficult to use, it might be because of one of the following two issues: VoiceOver is poorly supported, or simply the UX of your app might not be great and you should revisit that. If it takes effort to navigate the app with VoiceOver, it probably takes effort visually too and you may need to clean the interface up a bit, remove some clutter, add some headings, or better structure your content... Or if something sounds in the wrong order when navigating with VoiceOver, it might be because that UI component is not visually in the right place either.

Accessibility should be embedded in the team's culture and processes, but, as with any other software development process, the QA step might be the last chance to find any issues before it gets shipped to your users. So please, remember to use some of these techniques or tools to make sure your new feature is accessible before moving that ticket to done. And actually, if your team has a definition of done for a task in development, it would be an excellent idea to add "Accessible" as one of the requisites.

Shortcuts

Having Accessibility Shortcut enabled in your testing devices is a great way for having a quick access to the options you use the most. For a quick refresher on how to enable those both from your home/side button and in Control Center, you can go to the second chapter.

Accessibility Inspector and Environment Overrides

Before releasing an app or a new update, it is a good idea to test the final result in real devices for testing a closer experience to the one the final user will get. But while developing, it is sometimes just more convenient to use the simulator. There is a really useful tool embedded in Xcode that for some reason most people don't know about, the Accessibility Inspector. To open it, go to Xcode's top menu, and then Open Developer Tool, where you'll find very valuable tools like Instruments and, of course, the Accessibility Inspector (Figure 7-1).

Figure 7-1. *Accessibility Inspector*

Accessibility Inspector

The Accessibility Inspector makes it easy to test and find accessibility issues in your app. There are three main sections: one that will help you inspect the app, another one that will run an accessibility audit in the current screen of the app, and another one that will let you simulate different settings in your device.

Inspect: When inspecting your app, you can have a quick look at how the main accessibility properties are configured in your UI components, including the label, value, traits, or identifier.

New with Xcode 11, Apple has introduced a new feature for testing VoiceOver that comes very handy. If you click the icon with the speaker, you will be able to hear how VoiceOver would vocalize your app, you can go to the next and previous elements, or you can just click play and it will automatically start reading all the elements in your screen.

Audit: To run the accessibility audit in your app, just switch to the warning icon in the inspector, navigate in the simulator to the screen you'll like to audit, and click "Run Audit". When doing that, you'll get a list of potential issues. It even highlights where the potential issue is in the screen, and, if you click the little help icon, it will even hint a suggestion on how to fix it (Figure 7-2).

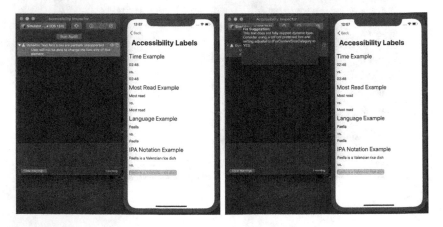

Figure 7-2. *Audit option with a warning (left) and a fix suggestion (right)*

The audit will help you catch a series of accessibility issues, including small-hit areas, non-accessible elements, text that does not support Dynamic Type, contrast ratio issues, images that contain the file name as its accessibility label, etc.

If you are starting to make your app more accessible, running one of these audits in your app is a great way of breaking the ice and starting to fix any issues it may have.

When dealing with contrast ratios, there is a hidden tool called "Color Contrast Calculator" (Figure 7-3) in the Accessibility Inspector in Window, in the top menu, which can be very useful too.

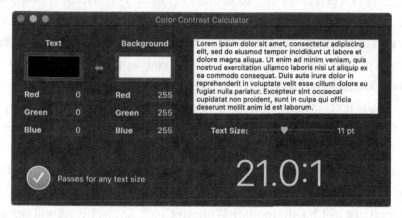

Figure 7-3. *Color Contrast Calculator tool*

For small-hit areas, make any tap targets at least 44pt x 44pt. Anything smaller than that will be just too small. You'll find users trying to action the button and failing most of the times. Does it sound familiar? Not a great experience, it is really frustrating! And it can make the app very difficult to use by people with tremors, shaking of the hands, or any other motor impairment, and also for users with low vision.

Settings: You'll find a few accessibility settings you can simulate in your iOS simulator, including Increase Contrast, Reduce Transparency, and Reduce Motion. Invert Colors will invert the colors of any images in your app, so you can see if they would be inverted or not when using Smart Invert Colors. But the tool in this section I find more useful by far is the possibility to tweak the font size and to see how the app reacts to those changes.

However, it may now exist a more convenient way to access some of these settings when testing your app. New in Xcode 11, you can use Environment Overrides.

Environment Overrides

Environment Overrides is new to Xcode 11 (Figure 7-4). When running your app in the simulator, you'll find a new option next to the Debug Memory Graph and the Debug View Hierarchy options. In this version, it has three sections. The first one allows you to see how your app would look in the new Dark Mode introduced in iOS 13. The second one, Text, will allow you to change the text size, the same way you could do with the Accessibility Inspector. The third one is all about Accessibility. You'll find some of the same options you can use in the Inspector too, like Increase Contrast, Reduce Motion, or Reduce Transparency, but also new ones like Bold Text, On/Off Labels, Button Shapes, or Grayscale, and a new accessibility setting introduced in iOS 13, Differentiate Without Color. Smart Invert will work as it does in your device instead of just inverting the images, which is what you get with the Accessibility Inspector at the moment.

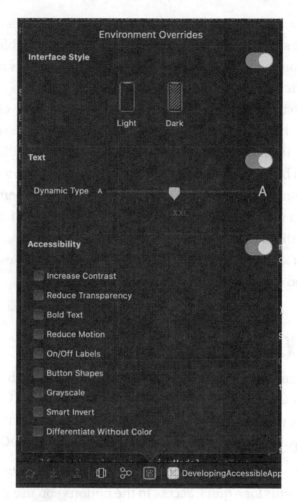

Figure 7-4. System Overrides menu

Switch control

There are plenty of ways for testing Switch Control. The easiest one
might be by connecting a Bluetooth keyboard to your device. Under the
Accessibility settings, you can enable Switch Control and also select how
many switches you want and what each of those does. For example, you
could configure just one switch and map it to the space bar of the keyboard

to select an item. This would let Switch Control scan the screen, and you could press the space bar when you wanted to select the highlighted element. But you can also have two switches: one that moves to the next item and another one to select it, for example.

But Apple has made things even easier for you to test. If you don't have an external Bluetooth keyboard, you can also configure switches that get triggered at the movement of your head. For example, a Right Head Movement can be used to select an item and even touches on the screen. However, this one will disable any other touches on the screen, so you may want to have an alternative switch and Accessibility Shortcut for an easy way to enable/disable Switch Control.

Have a quick browse to the settings menu; the possibilities for configuring and tweaking Switch Control are endless.

Summary

- Screen Curtain is the best way to test your app with VoiceOver and better empathize with your users. A triple tap with three fingers will turn off your screen, but you will still be able to use your app with VoiceOver.

- It is very convenient to configure some accessibility shortcuts for a quick access to the options you use the most.

- The Accessibility Inspector is a great tool that helps you find accessibility issues and test accessibility options in the simulator.

- There is a Color Contrast Calculator tool that will help you check if you have enough contrast ratio in the different parts of your app.

- Environment Overrides is a new feature in Xcode 11 that helps you easily test your app in the simulator, simulating different setting configurations, including some important accessibility settings.

- Don't forget to test with Switch Control. It is very easy to configure a keyboard as a switch.

Now we know a few ways to identify accessibility issues and check if our fixes work properly. It is time to try to find time to improve the accessibility of your apps by embedding accessibility in the day-to-day process of your team and company.

CHAPTER 8

Wrapping up

In this final chapter, I'd like to discuss where to go from here, where to get more resources, how to get involved in the community, and how to contribute to open source projects. There is so much to do! And we can help each other.

Accessibility in your team's culture

When speaking with other developers and teams about accessibility, most of the questions I get are around how to improve the culture around accessibility in the team and the company in general. It is definitely a very valid point. You are not going to be able to do it alone. One developer can't use their own spare time to make the app accessible, overview that the designs provided for new features are accessible, double-check that nothing has broken before a release in terms of accessibility… It is just not going to work.

It definitely needs to be a team effort. Everyone in the team needs to get some basic training to be aware that, like usability, testing, or security, accessibility is just part of your everyday set of things to take into account when developing digital products. And I am not talking about expensive certified trainings but just publicly sharing what everyone knows about it with the rest of the team and learn from each other. I will try to help you introduce accessibility in your team's culture by providing examples of things that I think have worked pretty well in different teams I have worked in.

© Daniel Devesa Derksen-Staats 2019
D. D. Derksen-Staats, *Developing Accessible iOS Apps*,
https://doi.org/10.1007/978-1-4842-5308-3_8

Please don't get frustrated; like every big change in a team's culture and ways of working, this will not change in a couple of days. It will take time and persistence. At times it may feel you are alone, but I promise it will pay off. The rest will eventually follow you because as we have seen it is just the right thing to do, and it will feel great. Here are a few things that can help you start making accessibility an essential part of your development process.

How good/bad is it?

A first step is to assess the situation. Identify what things can be improved in general, and which are the parts of the app that are in a worse shape and need more work. And document everything. Create a document in whatever documentation service your company uses, so it can be easily shared with the rest of your teammates. This has a few benefits. The first one is that it is a very visual way of communicating how good/bad your app is in terms of accessibility. If the list is very long, bad sign, if on the other hand it is short, you have probably been doing a great job. The other main benefit of documenting this is that when a colleague says something on the lines of "I would like to help but don't know where to start," you can redirect them to the document. They can probably start with the part of the app that they feel more familiar with and start fixing issues one by one. I usually divide the document in sections representing the different screens of the app and maybe even subviews if they're quite complicated and they deserve their own subsection. When solving an issue, I usually don't delete it from the list but either cross it out or add a symbol like a green check next to it to see that it has been fixed. It serves a bit as a history to see what things have been fixed lately, but more importantly it gives you a sense of progress; it is very gratifying to start crossing things out of the list.

When to do something like this is a different question. Ideally you have some time allocated, maybe even time-boxed, to do a first audit. But it might not always be easy to get the decision makers in your team buy into the idea of you spending time doing this kind of work. At least initially. So, I have done it in the past either when the company has given me time to do something that is not necessarily in the backlog, the famous 20 or 10% times, or more easily, whenever you are blocked for a few minutes. You can put your headphones on, turn VoiceOver on, and start navigating your app trying to go through the most important flows of your app from beginning to end. We all have times when the app is taking ages to compile, the project to clone or check out, we are waiting for some assets, the CI is down, etc.

And again, I mention VoiceOver because it is usually the most overlooked way of using your app and because improvements in VoiceOver can benefit some other of your users like Switch Control or Voice Control users. But please, go ahead and use the Accessibility Inspector too to find things like low-contrast ratio text with its background, small tappable areas, lack of support for Dynamic Type, etc. And also use your knowledge and intuition for anything that can be improved like spotting information that uses just color to convey important information, or finding some text that seems difficult to understand or too jargony and that could be simplified so it is easier to understand by everyone. Anything helps!

Next step: Share your findings

The next step in your master plan is to share your findings with as many people as you can. Pretty much everywhere I have worked in the past, there is usually some space where teams or individuals can share anything they want with the rest of the team, department, or company. It can be a sprint demo, an all-hands, town-hall, internal meetup, etc.

I find that live demos really help. If you have one, you can show a particularly bad use case that could be letting some of your users without the possibility of successfully using key features of your app. And then the magic is to show it fixed. As you have seen in this book, most of times those fixes take just a few lines of code. It is extremely eye-opening to see that going from non-usable to usable just took the determination to fix it and a dozen lines of code. No one will ever be able to say again that we can't afford doing it, that it is too difficult, or that we should first calculate the ROI or write a business case, because any of those things take more time than doing the actual work. It shouldn't actually require further justification.

Next, you can show them your document and invite anyone that would like to help to participate in it either helping with some of the issues or contributing with ideas to improve the general accessibility of the app.

Other small things you can do

And there is a wide range of things that you can do to make accessibility more important in your organization. Here you have a quick brainstorming of little things that can make a big difference:

- **Job descriptions**: You could try to find the person that writes the job descriptions for finding new iOS developers for your company and persuade them to add knowledge of accessibility as one of the requirements, or maybe one of the bonus point requirements for candidates. It is not about finding experts but showing that they care. If many companies do that, it will raise awareness among developers, and they will try to prepare accordingly when facing new interviews.

- **App release notes**: If your app is not great but you have been working on improvements, this is a great way of telling your users that you are working on it. They may give your app another chance or you might get some early feedback from them because they will know you will be happy to help with improvements. But again, it is about showing that you care, that you are willing to improve and to raise awareness. Figure 8-1 shows great examples from Halide or Skyscanner.

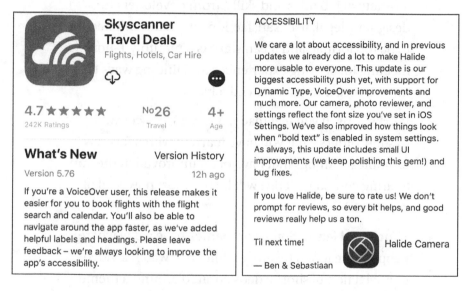

Figure 8-1. *App release notes*

- **Onboarding**: Do you have any onboarding documentation, tutorials, or workshops? It might be a great idea to add a small section about accessibility explaining why it is important to your team and how you work to create more accessible apps. One more reinforcement for new joiners so they know that it is part of the job.

- **Accessibility champions**: This may apply only for big teams or companies. If your company has guilds or any other way of bringing people with a strong interest about a particular topic, like a programming language, clean code, etc., together, you can create an accessibility group, if it doesn't exist yet, or join them if your company already has one. Ideally you would like to have a group as diverse as possible, and that includes at least one member of each team if possible and with a variety of job titles and skills, from developers to designers, legal, user satisfaction, etc. It doesn't need to be too formal, and it can start as a monthly 1-hour meeting for sharing experiences and finding ways to make a bigger impact collectively.

- **Workshops**: If you feel ready, it is really powerful to show others what you have learned with a few examples of things that have been improved in the app. Sharing your knowledge will be the most powerful of your tools!

- **Lunch and learn**: Some companies have a day where people have lunch together while they watch a video or a selection of short videos curated around a theme that someone shared to learn something new. If there is a lunch and learn session in your company, you can find interesting videos about accessibility that help raise awareness and inspire other people in your company. I totally recommend "Convenience for You is independence for Me"; it was one of the lunch sessions in WWDC 2017 where Todd Stabelfeldt told his story as someone who has lived with quadriplegia since the

age of 8 and how apps and technology changed his life
increasing his levels of autonomy: `https://developer.`
`apple.com/videos/play/wwdc2017/110/`.

Accessibility in your team's process

Now it is time to embed accessibility in your day-to-day process. And
this can slowly be done in a few different ways. In product discussions,
three amigos meetings, or any other chance you have to contribute to the
design of a new feature, keep your eyes open to propose any accessibility
improvements. Is the text too small or too light? Are some key actions
hidden behind complicated gestures? Are we offering closed captions
or subtitles for the new video player? And add some extra questions and
suggestions to the mix, so you or any of your colleagues make the feature
accessible without blockers, like: what does it look like when the user is
using the biggest accessibility font size? Or can we get some copy for this
button? It should just take a few repetitions of this process till everyone
realizes that those are things to take into account, so next time you may not
even have to keep asking for those that often.

The next step is code reviewing your peers' code. Have you spotted
anything in the code that could be improved to make your app more
accessible? Just add a comment to the PR and offer help to fix it if your
colleague doesn't have the skills to do it. Next time they will know.
I sometimes like to check out the branch and quickly run and test the
changes too. If you can catch any bug, it is much easier to fix at that stage.

And finally, if you have to run some manual testing or regression
testing of your app before releases, save a few minutes to check that
anything new is accessible and that what it was before hasn't regressed
either. Do you have a definition of done? Then you could include
"accessible" as one of the requirements. Or if you have a list of things your

team checks, and you have the power to propose changes to that, you can add an additional step to run the app using VoiceOver, for example. I'm sure QAs will be more than happy to help if you give them a hand and show them the best way of doing it.

Communities and meetups

One of the best ways to learn anything is to do it from another people's experience. I love going to meetups and conferences because you get to meet people with the same challenges and questions that you have and see how others are dealing with them.

I find this is especially true when it comes to accessibility where everyone is so passionate about it. We have talked about joining/creating an accessibility group at your workplace. But if there is not much expertise in your company right now, attending these meetups to learn a bit more from the talks and asking questions to people that may know a lot about it might be one of the best ways of quickly getting up to speed and learning from what worked and what didn't with others that are going through the same you are doing right now.

I would encourage you then to try to find your closest Accessibility Meetup. If you don't have one, don't worry. In London we have the London Accessibility Meetup, and they have a YouTube channel where they livestream their sessions and upload the videos of the talks after that. You may not have the networking and interaction bit that is so interesting, but at least you will be able to learn from the talks. And I am sure that most of the speakers will be happy to take questions through other channels like Twitter. I have learned so many things I wouldn't if it wasn't for this meetup like: what is an empathy lab, how to embrace inclusive design, how to design for users with aphasia, know more about the needs of your autistic users... And in general I learned a lot from people that work in organizations with a strong accessibility culture like the BBC or GDS (the Government Digital Service in the United Kingdom). The organizers do an amazing job trying to find people to tell their stories and bringing all us together every few weeks!

Where to go from here...

There are a ton of resources out there that you can use to learn more about the topic. Remember that you can find all the code examples from this book, and more, in this repo: `https://github.com/Apress/developing-accessible-iOS-apps`. Then, the first obvious place to go is Apple. This is their landing page: `www.apple.com/uk/accessibility/`, with a good overview of what Apple's platforms can offer for users with different abilities. Then, you can jump to the developers page: `https://developer.apple.com/accessibility/`, with access to all the videos from WWDC's technical sessions about accessibility since 2015, as well as the Design Guidelines and technical documentation.

There are also great talks about accessibility in many conferences. I've been really lucky to be given the opportunity to speak about it at Appdevcon, Altconf (where the idea of this book started!), SwiftFest (they had not just one but two talks about accessibility!), and Mobile Conf Th. I would recommend you any videos from Sommer Panage and Sally Shepard. I've learned so much from their talks. Here are a couple of my favorites:

- **Accessibility: A line of code can be many things**: `www.dotconferences.com/2018/01/sally-shepard-accessibility`

- **iOS Accessibility Tips & Tricks**: `https://youtu.be/dmMASdKhl_w`

There are other videos that are more informative about how assistive technology users use their devices and apps that will help you empathize better with their needs:

- **How Blind People Use iPhones**: `https://youtu.be/Hx4ivoI_GmM`

- **Convenience for You is independence for Me:** `https://developer.apple.com/videos/play/wwdc2017/110/`

And many blog posts, podcasts, or Twitter accounts... The Internet is full of great people trying to create more accessible apps! Just like you and me.

Spread the word!

Teach others what you've just learned. There is nothing more powerful to change a team's culture and to master a skill than to try to show others what you've just learned and how much of an impact it can make.

It has been an absolute pleasure to be able to write a bit about my experience in developing accessible iOS apps. I can't thank you enough for reading this book and I hope you enjoyed it. If you are now thinking of improving the accessibility of the apps you work on, that is mission accomplished! You can find me on Twitter as @dadederk. I'd love to hear about your thoughts and your experience or try to answer any questions you may still have. Let's do this!

Index

A, B, C

Accessibility
  automation tools and
    frameworks, 6
  benefits, 12, 114
  color vision deficiency, 5
  communities and meetups, 120
  design award winning apps and
    games, 7
  differences
    app release notes, 117
    job descriptions, 116
    lunch and learn, 118
    onboarding, 117
    teams/companies, 118
    workshops, 118
  element, 43, 44
  features, 3, 4
  hints, 42, 43
  inclusion and differences
    assistive technology, 9
    definition, 8
  labels
    abbreviations, 33, 34
    animations and spinners, 36
    buttons, 32, 33
    testing, 34–36

  learning, 26
  LED flash, 26
  legal agreement, 5, 6
  master plan, 115
  meaning, 1, 2
  Microsoft definition, 10, 12
  money, 4
  physical and motor, 22–26
  principles and techniques, 7
  resources, 121, 122
  screen reader, (*see* VoiceOver)
  self-rewarding, 7
  solutions benefit, 2
  team's culture, 113, 114
  team's process, 119
  technologies Apple offers, 14
  technology accessible, 10
  traits
    adjustable UI
      components, 40–43
    app information, 41
    button, 39
    header, 37, 38
  usability, 6
  user base, 3
  value, 42
  vision, 18

© Daniel Devesa Derksen-Staats 2019
D. D. Derksen-Staats, *Developing Accessible iOS Apps*,
https://doi.org/10.1007/978-1-4842-5308-3

Printed in the United States
By Bookmasters